IN HIM

Our Spiritual Blessings in Christ: A Study in the Book of Ephesians

F. Wayne Mac Leod

Light To My Path Book Distribution

Special thanks to the proofreaders:
Sue St. Amour, Lee Tuson

CONTENTS

About The Author

PREFACE

In the book of Ephesians, the apostle Paul communicates some wonderful truths to his readers about the blessings they have obtained through the work of the Lord Jesus on their behalf. I was struck some time ago, as I read this epistle at the reoccurrence of the phrase "in Him" or its equivalent in this epistle. This phrase is often repeated in connection with the blessings we have received from Christ as true believers.

I believe that we have often underestimated the power of what the cross of Christ accomplished in our lives. Until we understand what Christ has done, we will never truly be able to love and commit ourselves to Him in return.

The truths we will examine in this study are not new but they are life-changing. I trust you will not approach this book from an academic perspective. I did not write to communicate doctrine alone. My great desire is that the truth proclaimed in this study will have an impact on your relationship with Christ. This book is designed to be devotional in nature. That is to say, it is designed to help you to understand more about the Lord God and your relationship with Him.

I am fully aware that unless the Spirit of God applies this truth of this study it will have no lasting impact. My prayer is that this book would be used by the Holy Spirit in your life to strengthen, comfort and encourage you wherever you are in your walk with the Lord Jesus.

Over the next chapters, we will examine thirteen blessings we have received from the work of the Lord Jesus on our behalf. May these blessings become more real to you as you take the time to examine them and may they lift up your heart in praise and thanksgiving to Him who made this possible.

F. Wayne Mac Leod

1 - INTRODUCTION

Blessed be the God and Father of our Lord Jesus Christ, who has blessed us in Christ with every spiritual blessing in the heavenly places... (Ephesians 1:3)

Ephesians 1:3 is a summary of what I want to examine in the course of this study. It is also a summary of what the apostle Paul told the Ephesians in his epistle. My purpose in this work is not to write a commentary on Paul's letter to the Ephesians but rather to look briefly at what he told them about the blessings that were theirs "in Christ."

There is nothing new in what I am going to say. I suppose this is my greatest challenge as I embark on this study. We have all heard these truths before. The fact, however, is that I have often lost the wonder of what I have in Christ. The thing I admire about the apostle Paul is that he never seemed to lose that wonder. From the day he came to know the Lord to the last letter he wrote there is a sense of awe and amazement in what the Lord Jesus had done for him. I wish I had more of that attitude. How easy it is to take in the truth intellectually but not allow it to impact our hearts. My prayer is that as we examine Paul's teaching, we would come to a greater appreciation of what God the Father has done for us through His Son.

Paul begins his letter on a note of praise: "Blessed be the God and Father of our Lord Jesus Christ." I wish I could have been there when he was writing this letter. His heart seemed to explode with gratitude and praise to the Father for what He had done for him.

The Jewish people used the word "bless" to speak of praise and adoration. The Greek word used in this verse is the word *eulegetos*. It comes from the words *eu* meaning good and the word *logos* meaning word or speech. When the two words are put together, we get the sense of speaking well of someone. What Paul is saying in Ephesians 1:3 is something like this: May the God and Father of our Lord Jesus Christ be well spoken of. The reason for this is because of the blessings He had poured out through His Son Jesus. Paul's desire was for everyone who came to understand the blessings of the Father would speak well of Him and bring Him the praise that is due to His name. The result of these blessings was that God would be praised and blessed forevermore.

Notice something else from this verse. The praise goes to the Father. It is true that our blessings are the result of the work of the Lord Jesus, but in the mind of the apostle Paul, the Father also deserved great praise and glory. The blessings Paul speaks of come from the Father through the Son. While the Son paved the way for us to receive these blessings, their source is the heart of the Father. The Father has blessed us through the ministry of His Son.

Way before the Lord Jesus came to this earth it was the heart of the Father to restore it to Himself. It was the plan of God from the very beginning of time to send His Son to die for our sin. He was working out His purposes to draw a people to Himself who would bring Him praise and glory. Neither Satan nor sin would defeat that purpose. Jesus came to this earth because it was the Father's heart that He do so. Jesus was the Father's gift to a sinful and lost world. The Father sent His Son out of love for humanity. Jesus lovingly came in obedience to the Father. Paul gives thanks here to the Father. He recognizes that He also had a very important part to play in the blessings that would be ours through His Son.

While the Father is the source of all our spiritual blessings, these blessings are made possible through His Son Jesus Christ. Jesus came to die so that our sins could be forgiven and the purpose of the Father worked out in our lives. Sin was the obstacle. It kept us separated from God and under His judgment. Jesus' death paid the penalty for sin, brought forgiveness and healed our relationship with the Father. Now, all who come to the Father through the work of His Son can know the fullness of His blessing.

BY HIS STRIPES WE ARE HEALED
i.e OUR RELATIONSHIP WITH GOD is
BEING RESTORED.

Paul tells us in Ephesians 1:3 that the Father, through the Son, has now showered on us "every spiritual blessing in the heavenly places." Heaven is now opened up and all its blessings are made available to the believer. There will be no lack for those who are in Christ Jesus. God's provision will be equal to every problem or calling.

Notice, however, that Paul speaks about spiritual blessings. This is important. There is a sense in which all creation is blessed by God. Even those who do not believe in Him receive life and breath. The unbeliever lives his or her life on this earth, has the blessing of bearing children, friends, and experiences the many pleasures this life offers. These things are the result of God's blessing on all His creation.

Paul speaks here, however, about spiritual blessings. His focus is not on fine homes, nice cars or money in the bank. These are blessings from God but they are not the type of blessing Paul got excited about. What caused the apostle to praise the Father of our Lord Jesus Christ were the "spiritual blessings" he experienced which were the direct result of the ministry of Christ whom the Father had sent. This will be the focus of this study.

For Consideration:

What does this passage teach us about the role of the Father in our spiritual blessing and salvation?

What is the role of the Son in the blessings the Father

wants to give?

What is the difference between material blessings and spiritual blessings?

For Prayer:

Take a moment to thank the Father for His great heart of compassion for you. Thank Him that He sent His son to die for us.

Thank the Lord Jesus for His willingness to be the instrument through which the blessings of the Father could be brought to us.

Take a moment to consider the material blessings God has given to you. Thank Him for those material blessings.

Consider the spiritual blessings God has given you. Ask the Lord to give you a greater understanding of those blessings as you continue this study.

2 - CHOSEN BEFORE CREATION

3 Praise be to the God and Father of our Lord Jesus Christ, who has blessed us in the heavenly realms with every spiritual blessing in Christ. 4 For he chose us in him before the creation of the world to be holy and blameless in his sight. (Ephesians 1:3-4)

As we examine the blessings we have in Christ, the apostle begins in verse 4 by telling us that we were chosen in Christ "before the creation of the world to be holy and blameless in His sight." The Greek word used for "chosen" is the word eklegomai which literally means to select, to choose or to pick out. The word is used several times in the Scripture. Consider the following example:

Listen, my beloved brothers, has not God chosen those who are poor in the world to be rich in faith and heirs of the kingdom, which he has promised to those who love him? (James 2:5)

Notice from James 2:5 that God has *chosen* the poor in the world to be rich in faith and heirs of the kingdom. James tells us here that it was the decision of God that men and women, who were separated from Him, be forgiven and become heirs to the blessings of His kingdom. None of us would have known the salvation of God had He not chosen to open the doors of His kingdom to us.

The sad reality, however, is that while God calls many to this kingdom and its blessings, only a *chosen* few will be part of it.

> *For many are called, but few are chosen."* *(Matthew 22:14)*

The message of the gospel goes out to all people but only a few accept that message and come to faith in the Lord Jesus. As I examine my life and heart, I am forced to ask: How did I come to know the Lord Jesus and His salvation? Was it because I was more humble than the unbeliever next door? Was it because I grew up in a Christian home? Was it because I was more spiritual or intelligent than my neighbour? I know that none of these things are true. I came to faith in Christ only because the Holy Spirit pursued me and won my heart. If it were not for His work in my life, I would never have come to know Christ and the salvation He brought. I may have intellectually understood the truth about Jesus and salvation, but I would never have become a child of God. I owe this miracle to the purpose of God from the beginning of time, the work of Christ on the cross and the specific work of God's Holy Spirit bringing conviction and new life to my heart.

Why did the Holy Spirit choose to pursue me until He won my heart? Why did He put so much effort into my life? All I can say is that the Father loved me and had a purpose for my life. The Holy Spirit opened my heart and mind and made me a child of God. All I did was surrender to what God's Spirit was doing in me. If God had not chosen to pursue me and bring me to Himself, I would still be lost in my sin.

Elijah the prophet grieved over the fact that so many people had rejected the message he brought. He cried out to God about the prophets they had killed and how the people of his day had violently opposed the truth of God's word. Listen to what God told Elijah as recorded in Romans 11:2-6:

2 God has not rejected his people whom he foreknew. Do you not know what the Scripture says of Elijah, how he appeals to God against Israel? 3 "Lord, they have killed your prophets, they have demolished your altars, and I alone am left, and they seek my life." 4 But what is God's reply to him? "I have kept for myself seven thousand men who have not bowed the knee to Baal." 5 So too at the present time there is a remnant, chosen by grace. 6 But if it is by grace, it is no longer on the basis of works; otherwise grace would no longer be grace. (Romans 11:2-6)

In Elijah's despair, God told him that He had kept seven thousand men who had not bowed the knee to Baal. It was by the choice of God that these individuals had been kept from evil. The lesson Paul drew from this was that even in the present time, God has a "remnant, *chosen* by grace" that He has kept for Himself. His hand is on them, watching over them. His Spirit is pursuing and keeping them for the glory of God.

The message of salvation and a relationship with God would be completely rejected were it not for the work of the Holy Spirit in pursuing individuals, "chosen by grace", and bringing them to faith in Christ. Have you come to know the Lord Jesus as your Saviour today? Are you a child of God? This blessing is a result of the choice of God, first, to open up His kingdom to you and second, to pursue you, breaking all resistance and changing you from the inside. Every spiritual blessing I know is the result of this choice of God to bring me to Himself and make me His child.

Paul tells the Ephesians several things about this choice of God in Ephesians 1:4: Notice first, that they were chosen "in Christ." The Father's choice to make us His children was through the work of the Lord Jesus. He paid the penalty for our sin. He opened the door for us to become children of God. God's choice to make us His children was a costly one. It came at the price of His dear Son on the cross. He willingly paid that price, however, to restore us to Himself.

Notice second that God chose us before the creation of the world. This means that even before I was born,

God had a purpose for my life. His hand was on me from my conception. He chose to pursue me, planning and orchestrating the circumstances of my life so that I could become His child and know the fullness of fellowship with Him. Isaiah the prophet spoke of this when he said in Isaiah 49:1-3:

> 1 Listen to me, O coastlands, and give attention, you peoples from afar. The Lord called me from the womb, from the body of my mother he named my name. 2 He made my mouth like a sharp sword; in the shadow of his hand he hid me; he made me a polished arrow; in his quiver he hid me away. 3 And he said to me, "You are my servant, Israel, in whom I will be glorified." (Isaiah 49:1-3)

Notice how the Lord called Israel from its womb. Even before he was born, God had a purpose for his life. He had called and set him apart for a special purpose. The same was true of the apostle Paul. Notice what he told the Galatians in Galatians 1:13-17:

> 13 For you have heard of my former life in Judaism, how I persecuted the church of God violently and tried to destroy it. 14 And I was advancing in Judaism beyond many of my own age among my people, so extremely zealous was I for the traditions of my fathers. 15 But when he who had set me apart before I was born, and who called me by his grace, 16 was pleased to reveal his Son to me, in order that

I might preach him among the Gentiles, I did not immediately consult with anyone; 17 nor did I go up to Jerusalem to those who were apostles before me, but I went away into Arabia, and returned again to Damascus. (Galatians 1:13-17)

The apostle Paul was very much aware of the choice of God to bring Him to Christ and use Him to preach to the Gentiles. In fact, Paul never did seek Christ. He hated Christians and was on his way to Damascus to persecute them. He violently resisted Jesus and all He stood for. On that road to Damascus, the Lord struck Him down and changed his heart. If it had been up to Paul, he would have continued his persecution of the church but God had another plan for him. Paul tells us in Galatians 1 that God had actually set him apart before he was born. That purpose was not revealed to Paul until God chose to reveal His Son Jesus to him on the Damascus road.

Before time began, God had a purpose. That purpose included you and me. In His time, God would bring us into this world, reveal Himself to us and use us as His instruments to accomplish that plan.

Notice finally that God chose us before creation to be holy and blameless before Him. As God looked on the earth in the days of Noah, He saw that the heart of man had become desperately wicked and that all his thoughts were only evil (Genesis 6:5). Humanity was trapped in sin. From the beginning of time, God chose to rescue a people out of this evil by sending His Son. He would forgive their sin and place His Holy Spirit in them to keep them and enable them to walk as Christ walked. These people would be blameless and holy, not because they were perfect in themselves, but because the Lord Jesus would pay for their sin by His death on the cross of Calvary.

The cross of Christ was not an afterthought. Sin did not take God by surprise and send Him scrambling to find an answer. Even before creation, God had a people in mind. He would give them life and put them on this earth. He would save them from their sin and place His Holy Spirit in them to be His witnesses in a dark and sinful world. They would be a shining example of holiness to this world.

Do we really understand the incredible blessing that is ours in Christ? I would be lost in my sin and destined for an eternity of separation from God were it not for the choice of God to pursue me and bring me to Himself. I own my salvation to the Lord God, who before I was even born, chose to make me His child. I was born for a purpose. Even before I knew myself, my heavenly Father already knew me and had a purpose for my life. I was chosen "in him before the creation of the world to be holy and blameless in his sight" (Ephesians 1:4).

For Consideration:

What does it mean to be chosen by God? Answer this in regards to salvation and also in regards to service.

How much of our salvation can be attributed to ourselves and how much must be attributed to God and His choice to reach out to us?

Paul tells us that we were chosen before the creation of the world. What does this teach us about God's purpose for our lives?

What are our obligations to God knowing that He chose us before creation to be holy and blameless before Him as His servants?

What encouragement do you find in the fact that God's hand was on you from the moment of conception?

For Praise:

Take a moment to thank the Lord that He chose to open His kingdom to you. Thank Him that He pursued you until He won your heart.

Ask the Lord to help you understand the purpose He has for your life. Ask Him to help you to be faithful to that purpose.

Thank the Lord that His purpose for us was made possible not only through the choice of the Father but also at the cost of His Son's life and the work of His Spirit.

3 - PREDESTINED FOR ADOPTION AS SONS

In love, he predestined us for adoption as sons through Jesus Christ, according to the purpose of his will, to the praise of his glorious grace, with which he has blessed us in the Beloved. (Ephesians 1:4-6)

Paul told us in the last chapter that the Lord God chose us before the foundation of the world to be blameless and holy before Him. He goes on to tell us in Ephesians 1:4-6 that we were also predestined for adoption as sons through Jesus Christ.

There has been much debate throughout the history of the church over the role of God in this world and in the life of the individual. There are those who believe that God created the world and left it in human hands. They teach that we determine the course of our lives and the shape of our future.

It is true we make many decisions that determine the shape and texture of our lives. The fact of the matter, however, is that while we are free to make our decisions, God is still very much involved in the course of history. Someone compared this to a fish aquarium on a large ship. Inside the fish aquarium, the fish are making all kinds of decisions. They move from one place to another interacting with other fish. As they live out their lives in that aquarium, however, there is a greater force at work. The ship moves through the waters heading for a very particular destination. This is how it is with God. He is moving the flow of history toward its ultimate purpose. Kings and rulers, like fish in an aquarium, are making one decision after another but the ship of life continues to move in the direction God has determined.

There is something very comforting in knowing that there is someone above all the decisions we make. News reports show us that we do not always make wise decisions. One nation wars against another. Murder, immorality, and greed impact our societies. What hope would we have if there was no God in control? While God gives us the freedom to make decisions, He does not remove His hand from this world. In love, He moves the flow of history to accomplish His purposes for good.

I am so thankful that the Lord God has a plan for my life. While I know that I am free to make personal decisions in life, I am thankful that He cares enough to overrule my decisions. Imagine what would happen if your young child was free to make any decision he or she wanted without supervision. Young children do not have the maturity or understanding of life to always make wise decisions. A good parent watches over his or her child, overruling the decisions that hinder the safety or blessing of that child. My Heavenly Father cares for me in a similar way. As mature as I may be in my spiritual life, I still need His guidance and direction. I am dependent on Him to lead and keep me in His purposes.

This involvement of God in the affairs of humankind is seen in Ephesians 1:5 where Paul tells us that the Lord God predestined me for adoption. The word "predestined" comes from two Greek words. The first word *pro* simply means before. The second word *horizo* has the sense of marking something out, appointing or ordaining. The word used by Paul in verse 5 implies that God predetermines the course of history and will act to accomplish that purpose.

Notice that God predestined us for adoption. Adoption is the process whereby potential parents take a child who is not naturally born to them and makes that child their own with all the rights and privileges. Paul's use of the word, adoption, shows us that we were not naturally born as children of God. We do not become a child of God by natural birth. This is what Jesus said in John 3:6:

That which is born of the flesh is flesh, and that which is born of the Spirit is spirit.

We become children of God when He adopts us and accepts us as His own. God loved you before you loved Him. He took all the steps necessary to make this adoption possible. His Son died to pay the adoption price. His Spirit came to seal the relationship. All this took place before I was even aware of His presence. It was His decision to take a child that was not naturally His and adopt him as His own.

Notice that God chose to adopt us "as sons." This adoption makes us children of God. There are three things that come with our adoption as sons of God.

First, as sons and daughters of God, we have an obligation toward Him. We represent Him in everything we do. The writer to the Hebrews tells us that God will discipline His children who do not pursue His purpose for their lives:

> 5 And have you forgotten the exhortation that addresses you as sons? "My son, do not regard lightly the discipline of the Lord, nor be weary when reproved by him. 6 For the Lord disciplines the one he loves, and chastises every son whom he receives." 7 It is for discipline that you have to endure. God is treating you as sons. For what son is there whom his father does not discipline? 8 If you are left without discipline, in which all have participated, then you are illegitimate children and not sons. (Hebrews 12:5-7)

As a loving Father, God takes on the responsibility of

teaching and disciplining those who belong to Him. This discipline is not intended to harm us but to be a rich blessing for us. Were it not for the correction of the Lord God, we would never know the fullness of His blessing and purpose in our lives. As adopted children, we are corrected for our good and God takes it on Himself to shape us into His image.

Second, as adopted children of God, we participate in all the privileges of God's children. Paul speaks of this in Romans 8:16-17:

16 The Spirit himself bears witness with our spirit that we are children of God, 17 and if children, then heirs—heirs of God and fellow heirs with Christ, provided we suffer with him in order that we may also be glorified with him.

Paul told the Romans that as adopted children of God they were heirs of God and fellow heirs with Christ. They would know God's presence. They would know His strength, His gifts, and His wisdom. They would experience His comfort and His leading in what He had called them to do. Death would lose its power over them. It was only a stepping stone into the presence of their Heavenly Father. There in His presence, they would be free from the effects of sin and evil. There would be no more tears, pain or death (see Revelation 21:1-4). As adopted children of God, we are heirs to great blessing and privilege.

Third, as adopted children of God, we can experience

rich fellowship with God. Romans 8:14-15 speaks of this when the apostle Paul says:

14 For all who are led by the Spirit of God are sons of God. 15 For you did not receive the spirit of slavery to fall back into fear, but you have received the Spirit of adoption as sons, by whom we cry, "Abba! Father!"

The words, "Abba! Father!" reveal a special relationship between the child and the Father. Not everyone knows this special relationship. For many, God is distant. For those of us who have been adopted into the family of God, we know Him as a tender and compassionate Father. We can go to Him in our time of need. He keeps us and protects us from harm. He is deeply concerned for us and watches over us all the time. We can speak to Him at any time and be assured of His provision for our need.

What Paul tells us in this verse is that as believers we have been predestined for adoption. In its basic sense, this means that God, in His rich compassion and wisdom, loved us and determined to adopt us as His very own children. He decided, even before we knew Him, that He would shower His special love on us by making us His children and giving us all the privileges of heaven.

I did not deserve this privilege. Were it not for the fact that He determined to adopt me as His child, I would still be lost in my sin and separated from Him forever. I owe this to God and His willingness to accept me and make me His child. What greater blessing could there be than to be chosen by God and adopted as His very own?

For Consideration:

What comfort do you find in the fact that the Lord God is still involved in the events of this life? What would happen if He did not overrule what took place in this world?

What comfort do you find in the fact that God watches over you and overrules your decisions and circumstances?

Were you born into this world as a child of God? What does the doctrine of adoption teach us about becoming children of God?

What does it mean to be adopted?

What are the privileges and obligations of the adopted children of God?

For Prayer:

Thank the Lord that He does not leave us to ourselves but overrules circumstances and events to accomplish His greater purpose.

Thank the Lord for His discipline which helps you to become all He intends you to be.

Thank the Lord the He chose to adopt you and make you His child. Thank Him for the love and compassion that made this happen.

Ask God to help you to live as an adopted child. Ask Him to give you the grace to walk in a manner worthy of your relationship with Him.

Take a moment to consider the many privileges you have now because God has accepted you. Thank Him for what He has given you through Christ.

Thank the Lord that He is bigger than the worst situations in life.

4 - REDEMPTION

In Him we have redemption through His blood, the forgiveness of our trespasses, according to the riches of His grace. (Ephesians 1:7)

We have been examining what Paul taught the Ephesians about their blessings in Christ. The next blessing we have in Christ can be seen in Ephesians 1:7. Here Paul reminded the Ephesians that they had redemption through Christ's blood.

The word redemption, in its basic sense, refers to a payment made for something to be released. In many ways, it is a legal concept. When something is redeemed it is released from bondage, injustice, obligation or penalty. The result of this redemption is freedom. There are several assumptions we can make from Paul's use of the word redemption in this verse.

We Need To Be Released

The first assumption is that we need to be released. Listen to what the Lord Jesus said in John 8:34:

Jesus answered them, "Truly, truly, I say to you, everyone who commits sin is a slave to sin.

Speaking about himself, the apostle Paul said:

For we know that the law is spiritual, but I am of the flesh, sold under sin. (Romans 7:14)

Scripture teaches that we were slaves to sin. We were slaves in two ways. First, we were slaves to the lusts of sin. Paul was very honest about this struggle when he wrote:

18 For I know that nothing good dwells in me, that is, in my flesh. For I have the desire to do what is right, but not the ability to carry it out. 19 For I do not do the good I want, but the evil I do not want is what I keep on doing. (Romans 7:18-19)

The apostle recognized a struggle in his life. He wanted to serve the Lord but there was a force at work in him that kept him from becoming all God wanted him to be. That force was sin. Who among us does not struggle with our thoughts or words? We think and speak things that do not honour the Lord our God. We dare not do what comes naturally for us. Instead, we must struggle with our impulses, attitudes, and thoughts. Looking at the human race in the days of Noah, the Lord was grieved because its heart had become evil. Speaking of this in Genesis 6:5 the writer says:

The LORD saw that the wickedness of man was great
in the earth, and that every intention of the thoughts
of his heart was only evil continually.

We are slaves to the lusts of sin. Our hearts are attracted to sin. We are aware of its influence in our lives from a very early age.

We were not only slaves to the lusts of sin but Scripture teaches us secondly that we were also slaves to the penalty of sin. This is the very clear teaching of Paul in Romans 6:23 when he writes:

For the wages of sin is death, but the free gift of God is
eternal life in Christ Jesus our Lord.

Separation from God and His blessings is the penalty for sin. The result of sin is death. This death is a spiritual death in the present live and eternal separation from God in the life to come. This is a very serious matter. Every one of us has experienced this separation from God because of sin; there is no exception apart from the Lord Jesus.

For all have sinned and fall short of the glory of God
(Romans 3:23)

We were enslaved by sin's lust and penalty and need to be released from its power over our lives.

God is a God of Justice

The second point we need to see in Paul's use of the word redemption is that God submits Himself to a code of justice. Consider this for a moment. The Lord God is the Creator of the world. There is no one greater than Him. There is no higher court to which we can appeal. He sets the standards of truth and justice. No one can question His judgements. Why should the Creator God have to pay a redemption price to redeem us from the lusts and penalty of sin?

Scripture makes it abundantly clear that the Lord God is a God of justice (see Deuteronomy 32:4; Romans 3:26; John 5:30). Ephesians 1:7 tells us that through His Son, the Father redeemed us from sin. That is to say, He paid the penalty necessary to release us from the lusts and the penalty of our sin. Justice is a vital part of God's character. He will not override justice. The penalty of sin must be paid if we are to be released from its power and consequences. God maintains this code of justice and submits Himself to its standards.

Payment Is Required

The third detail we need to understand is that redemption requires a payment. There can be no release until the price has been paid. I remember speaking some time ago at a youth retreat. The parents were invited to the final chapel meeting. While I cannot remember the subject of my message that evening, I do remember one of the parents coming up to me later and saying: "I agree with what you were saying but one thing that has always puzzled me is all this talk about the blood of Christ. I have never understood why Christ had to die."

This question is still being asked in our day. Why did Jesus have to die? Wasn't there another way for us to be released from the penalty of sin? The answer to this question is rooted in the concept of justice. Injustice and evil must be punished. What would our society be like if we refused to punish criminals? Would there not be an outcry in our land? Crime demands a penalty.

Also rooted in our sense of justice is the idea that the more serious a crime is, the greater the penalty needs to be. We distinguish between a man who parks his car in a no parking zone and the person who murders another human being. To make a murderer pay a small fine for killing another human being would be as unjust as giving a life sentence in prison to a man who parked his car in a no parking zone. Justice demands that the penalty suit the crime. The question we need to ask ourselves now is this: What is the nature of our offense before God? To understand this we need to hear the judgment of God our judge in Romans 3:10-18:

> *10 as it is written: "None is righteous, no, not one; 11 no one understands; no one seeks for God. 12 All have turned aside; together they have become worthless; no one does good, not even one." 13 "Their throat is an open grave; they use their tongues to deceive." "The venom of asps is under their lips." 14 "Their*

mouth is full of curses and bitterness." 15 *"Their feet are swift to shed blood; 16 in their paths are ruin and misery, 17 and the way of peace they have not known."* 18 *"There is no fear of God before their eyes."*

Imagine for a moment a man being tried before a court. As the judge listens to the testimonies that come before him, he makes the following declaration. "I see this man to be a godless man. He has no fear of God. I find no evidence of anything good in him. He is a worthless excuse for a human being. He is a liar and a slanderer. He will murder anyone who gets in his way. Everywhere he goes he leaves misery and ruins."

Are these not serious accusations? These accusations come from the highest court. Listen again to the judgement of God in Genesis 6:5:

> *The Lord saw that the wickedness of man was great in the earth, and that every intention of the thoughts of his heart was only evil continually.*

"Every intention of the thoughts of his heart was only evil continually." Again this is a serious matter. Most of us just don't see this to be the case. Don't we also do good things? Aren't there some good thoughts in our heart? Obviously, our standard is very different from God's. As God looks at the human heart, He sees it from a completely different perspective:

9 The heart is deceitful above all things, and desperately sick; who can understand it? 10 "I the Lord search the heart and test the mind, to give every man according to his ways, according to the fruit of his deeds." (Jeremiah 17:9-10)

When God looks at the human heart and mind He sees it as "deceitful above all things, and desperately sick." In fact, the New International version of the Bible translates this with the phrase: "beyond cure." In other words, there is nothing that can be done about the evilness of the human heart. The capacity for every evil imaginable is found in the human heart. We have seen the fruits of the human heart in the history of this world. Violence of all kind takes root in the human heart. Every abuse and crime ever committed found fertile soil in the human heart. Take a moment to see the countless souls that have perished through wars and violence as nation rise up against nation. Pause for a moment to think about the abuses that have taken place in families. Listen to the news and ask yourself, where does all this injustice and violence come from? It comes from the human heart. My heart is not different from the person next to me. It feels the same temptations. It is as capable of as much evil as any criminal. I may not act on that evil, but it is still in my heart.

It is not without reason that the Lord God tells us that He will give us a *new* heart. Jesus did not come to fix our sinful hearts but to give us completely new ones. The old one was "beyond cure." Throughout Scripture, we are called to die to the flesh and its sinful desires.

And those who belong to Christ Jesus have crucified the flesh with its passions and desires. (Galatians 5:24)

Notice from Galatians 5:24 that we are to "crucify the flesh and its passions and desires." This means that God's intention is for us to kill the sinful nature. He does not come to fix this nature but to give us a new one. The sinful nature must be put to death.

What we learn from this is that the heart is beyond repair. It is the source of every evil under the sun. It must be put to death. The Lord God sentences the human heart to death for it has been the source of every sin and crime this world has ever known. It has rebelled against God and cannot be repaired.

Payment of the Redemption Price Brings Release

The final point we need to make here about Paul's use of the word redemption is that when the price is paid, the result is freedom and liberty. As human beings, we were under the sentence of death for our sin. We were born with hearts that were "desperately sick" and "beyond cure." In His infinite compassion and wisdom, however, the Lord God sent His only Son to pay the penalty for our sin. He took our penalty on Himself. He laid down His life on the cross so that justice would be served. He paid the ultimate penalty for our sin.

We have seen that we were slaves to both the penalty and to the lust of sin. Jesus took care of the penalty by His death on the cross. He also took care of our lust for sin as well. He did this by giving us a new heart. He promised to do this way back in the days of Ezekiel:

And I will give you a new heart, and a new spirit I will put within you. And I will remove the heart of stone from your flesh and give you a heart of flesh. (Ezekiel 36:26)

Paul describes this in 2 Corinthians 5:17:

Therefore, if anyone is in Christ, he is a new creation. The old has passed away; behold, the new has come.

Something wonderful happened the day we came to faith in Jesus Christ. He paid our penalty and gave us a new heart. We are no longer under God's wrath. The price has been paid so that we can be freed from the lust and penalty of sin. As children of God, chosen and adopted by the Father we have been redeemed at the cost of His Son's life so that we can be freed from the lust and penalty of sin. Because of this, we are a new creation.

For Consideration:

What is redemption? Why do we need it?

What do we learn here about God's commitment to justice?

What is the difference between how God sees us and how we see ourselves?

What did our redemption cost Christ?

What does redemption accomplish in our lives?

What evidence do you see in your life that you have been set free from the lust and penalty of sin?

For Prayer:

Ask the Lord to help you to accept His judgment of the human heart.

Thank the Lord that He was willing to pay the penalty for your sin.

Thank the Lord that He also sets us free from the lust of sin. Ask Him to help you to walk in the desires of the new heart He has given you.

5 - UNITED UNDER HIM

Making known to us the mystery of his will, according to his purpose, which he set forth in Christ as a plan for the fullness of time, to unite all things in him, things in heaven and things on earth. (Ephesians 1:9-10)

The next spiritual blessing the apostle Paul speaks about is found in Ephesians 1:10. Here in this verse, Paul told the Ephesians that the Father made known His will to unite all things in Christ. The English versions of the Bible translate this phrase differently. Each of these translations gives us a slightly different picture of Paul's meaning here. Consider the following translations of the phrase "to unite all things in him" in Ephesians 1:10:

... to bring all things in heaven and on earth together under one head, even Christ (NIV)

... bring everything together under the authority of Christ--everything in heaven and on earth. (NLT)

... the summing up of all things in Christ, things in the heavens and things on the earth. (NASB)

... gather together in one all things in Christ, both which are in heaven, and which are on earth; even in him. (KJV)

The word translated "unite" in the English Standard Version of the Bible is the Greek word "*anakephalaiomai.*" It comes from two root words. "Ana" can be translated by the words "between" or "in the midst of." The word "*kephalaioo*" has the idea of wounding someone on the head or "to bring under." It is a somewhat difficult word to understand. Remember, however, that to strike someone on the head is to deal a strong blow. That blow to the head will bring them into submission. When we put the two words together, we get the idea of Christ dealing a final blow that brings all things into submission to His Father's purpose. We need to consider this concept in greater detail and see how it relates to us as believers.

As we begin to examine this phrase, we need to remember the state of the world in which we live. Satan is described as being its master. Speaking to His disciples in John 14:30-31 Jesus said:

> *I will no longer talk much with you, for the ruler of*
> *this world is coming. He has no claim on me.*

Speaking about the ultimate judgment of Satan Jesus says in John 12:31:

> *Now is the judgment of this world; now will the ruler*
> *of this world be cast out.*

We see from this that Satan has been ruling in the hearts and minds of men and women on this earth. He has caused unending chaos and hurt. We cannot read or listen to the latest news reports without seeing evidence of his presence and rule. This world seems to be held in subjection to Satan and his ways. Wars and violence abound. Crimes of greed and passion show us that Satan has power over the minds and hearts of men and women all around us. What hope would there be for this world if nothing were done about its present ruler? Human beings would be trapped by sin and evil. Death and decay would reign everywhere. Men and women would live in fear with no hope. Despair and unending pain would be their only reality. Satan is a cruel master.

Paul tells us in Ephesians 1:10 that it is the purpose of God to unite all things in Him (that is, in Christ). As we have already seen, the word used here refers to bringing all things into submission to Christ and under His Lordship. The reason Jesus came to this earth was to defeat the power of Satan and to set up a kingdom where He (Christ) would be its leader.

One of the central teachings of Jesus is related to the coming of the Kingdom of God on earth (see Matthew 4:17; Mark 1:15). For that kingdom to be established, two things needed to take place. First, there was the matter of defeating the power of the current evil master. Satan had to be stopped. No one was able to do this but the Lord Jesus. The second matter to be addressed was the legal hold of Satan over his subjects. Sin was the contract that bound us to Satan. As long as the penalty of sin was not paid, we would always be under Satan's authority. Jesus came to pay the price for our sin so that Satan could no longer have any legal hold on us. Remember that God, as a God of justice, holds himself to a strict code of justice so this legal matter had to be addressed.

Satan's authority over us was defeated by the cross of Jesus Christ. All who belong now to Him have a new and loving master. This new master is very different from our old master. He is holy and kind. He guides and protects us as a Good Shepherd. He promises His presence and reminds us that all things will work together for good if we love Him and walk in His ways (Romans 8:28). He is preparing a home for us where we can live with Him. He will come and take us to be with Him forever (see John 14). There could not be a more loving and compassionate master. It is a privilege to be His servant and a citizen of His kingdom.

Because of His great work in defeating Satan and

establishing the Kingdom of God on this earth, the Lord Jesus was given a name that was above every other name.

9 Therefore God has highly exalted him and bestowed on him the name that is above every name, 10 so that at the name of Jesus every knee should bow, in heaven and on earth and under the earth, 11 and every tongue confess that Jesus Christ is Lord, to the glory of God the Father. (Philippians 2:9-11)

The father exalted the Lord Jesus. There is no greater name in heaven or earth than the name of the Lord Jesus Christ. He is the undisputed King. To Him, every knee, in heaven and earth must bow. Every tongue must confess Him as Lord of all. By His work on the cross, the Lord Jesus brings all things into submission to His Lordship. All who reject His Lordship will suffer the judgment of the Father.

What is the application of this truth to our lives today? There are several points we need to make in this regard.

Satan Has Been Conquered

The first encouragement we need to take from Ephesians 1:10 is that Satan has been conquered. He had been a dreadful master. Those who belong to the Lord Jesus, however, no longer are subject to him. His hold over us has been legally broken through the death of the Lord Jesus. He still tries to distract and tempt us but he has ultimately been conquered by Christ and we share in that victory.

Imagine that you were living in Bible times. Your king had gone out to fight a fearful enemy that was oppressing you for years. Now he is returning home. He rides his war horse into the city after a long but victorious battle. You join your fellow citizens along the streets of the city to welcome your king. He has set you free from your enemy. There is joy and great hope for the future, now that the enemy has been defeated. This is cause for celebration.

Christ's victory over Satan gives us cause for great rejoicing. We have hope now where once there was only despair. The darkness of separation from God gives birth to a new life through His Son. Death is no longer feared. It is a stepping stone into the presence of our loving Master. We were once oppressed and bound but now, under our new master, we are free from the penalty of sin to enjoy fellowship with our Creator. Sin, death, and Satan have all been conquered in the Lord Jesus. They have been struck on the head and brought into submission to His justice and headship.

New Master

Our new Master has our best interests at heart. He has a purpose for our lives. He longs to fellowship with us and takes a personal interest in our wellbeing. Service and life under this new Master is very different from our old master. We have the privilege of being His ambassadors in this world.

Therefore, we are ambassadors for Christ, God making his appeal through us. We implore you on behalf of Christ, be reconciled to God. (2 Corinthians 5:20)

No service under this new Master will go unrewarded.

And without faith it is impossible to please him, for whoever would draw near to God must believe that he exists and that he rewards those who seek him. (Hebrews 11:6)

The apostle Paul, as the time of his death drew near, looked forward to entering the presence of his Lord and Master and receiving his reward:

7 I have fought the good fight, I have finished the race, I have kept the faith. 8 Henceforth there is laid up for me the crown of righteousness, which the Lord, the righteous judge, will award to me on that Day, and not only to me but also to all who have loved his appearing. (2 Timothy 4:7-8)

Unlike our old master, whose only desire was to use us and destroy us, our new master gives us the privilege not only to serve Him but also to reign with Him.

If we endure, we will also reign with him; if we deny him, he also will deny us; (2 Timothy 2:12)

9 And they sang a new song, saying, "Worthy are you to take the scroll and to open its seals, for you were slain, and by your blood you ransomed people for God from every tribe and language and people and nation, 10 and you have made them a kingdom and priests to our God, and they shall reign on the earth." (Revelation 5:9-10)

What hope is ours now that our Lord has united us under his banner and lordship. Under His reign, we have the confidence to face the enemy. We can boldly serve our new Master for He provides all we need and seeks our good. Our new Master knows us personally and has a great purpose for our lives. We will reign with Him and enjoy His presence forever.

Christ came to unite a people under His authority and reign setting then free from the bondage of Satan our old master. What security there is now under Christ's headship! He is our King and Lord. He is our Guide and Protector. Under Him we are forgiven, cleansed, cared for and protected.

For Consideration:

How is Satan the ruler of this world? What evidence is there of his kingdom and reign?

How would you describe the rule of Satan on this earth? What are the characteristics of his rule?

What did the cross of Jesus do to free us from the bondage of Satan?

Why are people still under the dominion of Satan even after the death and resurrection of Christ?

Compare the rule of Satan with the rule of Christ. How do they differ as masters?

Have you come to Christ and asked Him to free you from the bondage of sin in your life? What difference has it made in your life to be under a new Master?

For Prayer:

Thank the Lord that He is able to overcome Satan and set us free from his bondage.

Ask the Lord to break the power of Satan in your community and in the lives of those you love.

Take a moment to give thanks to the Lord for the beauty of His reign in your life. Thank Him for how He cares for you as your Lord and Master.

If you have never accepted the work of Christ to free you

from the bondage of sin and Satan, take a moment now and ask Him to set you free.

Thank the Lord Jesus that He came to break the power of Satan and unite you with other brothers and sisters under the rule of the Father.

6 - AN INHERITANCE IN HIM

In him we have obtained an inheritance, having been predestined according to the purpose of him who works all things according to the counsel of his will so that we who were the first to hope in Christ might be to the praise of his glory. (Ephesians 1:11-12)

In Ephesians 1:11, Paul went on to tell the believers in Ephesus that they had received an inheritance in Christ Jesus. Before considering this inheritance, let's take a moment to consider the context of verses 11-12. There are four things we need to see in these two verses.

First, notice that we have received an inheritance *in Christ*. He is the means by which this inheritance comes to us. Without Christ, there would be no inheritance. He not only brings this inheritance to us from the Father but He is also the one who made it possible by means of His death. The inheritance we receive cost Jesus His life. For us to obtain this inheritance, Jesus had to leave the glories of heaven and live as a man. He suffered all that we suffer and ultimately died the cruel death of the cross. He was separated from His Father because of our sin. Our inheritance is in Christ alone. There is no other way to receive this inheritance but through the work and in the person of the Lord Jesus Christ.

The second point Paul makes in these verses is that we have already obtained this inheritance. Notice that Paul speaks to the Ephesians in the past tense: "we *have obtained* an inheritance." Admittedly, we have not experienced all there is of this inheritance but it is ours the moment we come to Christ. The papers have been signed and the matter is legally ours in Christ. We are already experiencing parts of this wonderful inheritance now in our lives. There is also much more to come. Our inheritance has both a present and a future reality but it is already ours.

Third, Paul tells us that our inheritance was the result of the Father's sovereign plan for our lives. Notice that he told the Ephesians that this was predestined according to God's purpose. This means that we did not obtain this inheritance because we deserved or earned it. God did not have to give us an inheritance but He determined from the beginning of time (before we were born) that He would. Our inheritance is a result of the gracious choice of God.

Finally, our inheritance is for the praise of God's glory.

It is true that we are richly blessed by this inheritance but so is God. God receives great praise from His people for His mercy toward them. For all eternity, we will give Him thanks for what He has done. There will never be enough time to express our gratitude for this inheritance. We will enjoy, for all eternity, the fullness of His blessing and praise His name. The angels of heaven marvel at this mighty and wonderful salvation.

Having seen what Paul told the Ephesians in verses 11-12, let's take a moment to consider what Scripture teaches us about our inheritance in Christ. Remember that Paul has been speaking about *spiritual* blessings in Christ. This tells us that the inheritance he is speaking about is a spiritual inheritance. Spiritual does not mean, however, that there will not be a physical aspect to this blessing. The inheritance of the believer, however, relates primarily to his or her salvation and the fruit of the salvation accomplished by Christ on the cross. Let's consider this briefly.

Our salvation through Christ is our great inheritance. This salvation has many implications in our lives. First, it brings us forgiveness of sin. Christ's death paid our penalty. This was a debt we could not pay. He died on the cross to pay our debt. What a wonderful sense of freedom the removal of debt brings. It releases us from obligation and sets us free from a tremendous burden. This was especially true in the case of sin. Sin was a cruel master. In Christ, we have been freed from its grip. This is an inheritance that is worth more than the whole world. Listen to what the Lord Jesus said about this in Matthew 16:26:

For what will it profit a man if he gains the whole world and forfeits his soul? Or what shall a man give in return for his soul?

You may inherit a great fortune in money and property but what good is that property to you in death? Would you not be willing to give up all you had if by doing so you could be assured that you would be freed from sin and its judgment?

Beyond the matter of forgiveness, however, is the relationship with God that is the inheritance of all believers. Consider what Paul told the Philippians in Philippians 3:7-10:

7 But whatever gain I had, I counted as loss for the sake of Christ. 8 Indeed, I count everything as loss because of the surpassing worth of knowing Christ Jesus my Lord. For his sake I have suffered the loss of all things and count them as rubbish, in order that I may gain Christ 9 and be found in him, not having a righteousness of my own that comes from the law, but that which comes through faith in Christ, the righteousness from God that depends on faith — 10 that I may know him and the power of his resurrection, and may share his sufferings, becoming like him in his death.

Paul told the Philippians that he was willing to give

up everything for the sake of Christ. He counted everything in this life to be a loss compared to knowing Christ Jesus. He considered everything rubbish compared to gaining Christ and knowing Him. Those who know this Christ find that the things of this world lose their attraction. The more they know Him, the more they are willing to surrender all they have to know Him more. There is no relationship as precious or intimate as a relationship with the Lord Jesus. This relationship is worth the entire world to obtain. The sweetness and intimacy of communion with Him cannot be compared to anything else in this world. It is of greater worth than all the wealth and treasures this world could give. Knowing Him satisfies our soul as nothing in this world ever could.

The inheritance of the believer is eternal life. This life, however, is not like anything we experience in this world. It is a life in the presence of our Lord and Saviour. It is a life free from sin and its fruit. It is a life under the fullness of His blessing. It is a life that fully satisfies. It is not our purpose in this study to get into all the details about heaven and eternal life. Suffice it to say that the richest inheritance we experience in this world cannot be compared to what is to come. Speaking to the Corinthians Paul said:

> But, as it is written, "What no eye has seen, nor ear heard, nor the heart of man imagined, what God has prepared for those who love him"— (1 Corinthians 2:9)

Notice that the human eye has never seen the kind of things God has prepared for those who love Him. The human ear has never heard of the things God has for His people. The heart of man could not even imagine the blessings in store for those who accept His Son. We have seen a lot of beautiful and marvellous things on this earth. In our wildest imagination, we have imagined incredible blessing but we can be assured of one thing; God will surprise us when we see Him in glory. We will be awestruck and amazed beyond measure at the things He has prepared for us.

In this life here below we are promised the presence of God who will never leave us. His comfort is our strength in trial. His mercy and forgiveness our hope in failure. His provision our source for every task He has called us to do. Time does not permit us to speak here of all these blessings but those who belong to Him know them on a daily basis. These and many more such blessings are the spiritual inheritance of all who are in Christ.

Let me conclude this reflection with some comments on the teaching of the rest of Scripture about the inheritance of the believer. Paul told the Ephesians that their inheritance could not be taken from them.

13 In him you also, when you heard the word of truth, the gospel of your salvation, and believed in him, were sealed with the promised Holy Spirit, 14 who is the guaranteed of our inheritance until we acquire possession of it, to the praise of his glory. (Ephesians 1:13-14)

Ephesians 1:14 tells us that the Holy Spirit is the guarantee of our inheritance. We will examine this point in greater detail in another chapter. Suffice it to say for the moment that while we may not always serve the Lord as we ought, God's promise remains. God signs this deal by putting His Holy Spirit in our lives. The Spirit of God in us is our guarantee that nothing can take this wonderful inheritance from us.

Our inheritance is not only guaranteed, but it is also an imperishable, undefiled and unfading inheritance:

> *3 Blessed be the God and Father of our Lord Jesus Christ! According to his great mercy, he has caused us to be born again to a living hope through the resurrection of Jesus Christ from the dead, 4 to an inheritance that is imperishable, undefiled, and unfading, kept in heaven for you, 5 who by God's power are being guarded through faith for a salvation ready to be revealed in the last time. (1 Peter 1:3-5)*

Peter says that our inheritance is "kept in heaven for you." It is ours in Christ. God keeps it particularly for us. If God keeps it for us, who will keep us from it? This inheritance is "imperishable, undefiled, and unfading." In other words, nothing will ever take it from us. No sin will ever defile or remove our delight in it. Its beauty will never fade away nor will our enjoyment of it.

God has been preparing this inheritance for us even before we were born. In fact, Jesus told us that He was preparing our inheritance from the very foundation of the world.

33 And he will place the sheep on his right, but the goats on the left. 34 Then the King will say to those on his right, 'Come, you who are blessed by my Father, inherit the kingdom prepared for you from the foundation of the world. (Matthew 25:34)

While we do not deserve this wonderful inheritance, Paul told the Colossians that God qualified them to share in it with all the saints of light:

12 giving thanks to the Father, who has qualified you to share in the inheritance of the saints in light. 13 He has delivered us from the domain of darkness and transferred us to the kingdom of his beloved Son, 14 in whom we have redemption, the forgiveness of sins. (Colossians 1:12-14)

Notice that it was God who qualified us for this inheritance. We did not qualify ourselves. God made us qualify by sending His Son to forgive and rescue us from Satan's grip. We owe our inheritance completely to Him.

As we conclude our reflection on Ephesians 1:11-12, we need to see the incredible grace of God that qualified us by means of the death of His Son to receive such an inheritance. We cannot possibly understand in this life the immensity of this inheritance. Even now we struggle to fully understand the blessings of forgiveness and a relationship with God. How much more difficult is it to understand the fullness of that blessing in heaven? May the Lord give us greater insight, by means of these verses, to understand more fully the tremendous inheritance of forgiveness, relationship with God and eternal life in His gracious and loving presence. This and much more has been prepared for us as our inheritance in Christ.

For Consideration:

How can we experience the inheritance God offers? What is the qualification for this inheritance?

Do any of us qualify naturally for this inheritance?

What would you give to know the forgiveness of your sin and a right relationship with God?

Can our inheritance be taken from us?

What keeps us from experiencing the beauty of our inheritance now?

Can we truly understand the fullness of our inheritance in this life?

What parts of this inheritance have you been

experiencing in the past few months?

For Prayer:

Take a moment to thank the Lord God that He made us qualify for our inheritance by means of the work of His Son.

Thank God for the forgiveness He offers through the work of His Son Jesus.

Ask the Lord to help you to experience and understand the fullness of inheritance He has given you in and through the work of Christ.

Thank the Lord for what you are currently experiencing of your inheritance right now.

7 - SEALED BY THE HOLY SPIRIT

13 In him you also, when you heard the word of truth, the gospel of your salvation, and believed in him, were sealed with the promised Holy Spirit, 14 who is the guarantee of our inheritance until we acquire possession of it, to the praise of his glory. (Ephesians 1:13-14)

As Paul continues his teaching on the spiritual blessings of the believer, he told the believers in Ephesus that they were sealed with the Holy Spirit as a guarantee of their inheritance (Ephesians 1:13-14). Notice particularly that this sealing only took place when the Ephesians heard and believed the "the word of truth, the gospel of your salvation." This tells us that the sealing of the Holy Spirit is only for believers.

We need to be careful not to confuse a general work of the Holy Spirit with the sealing that Paul speaks about here. The Spirit of God can use whomever He pleases to accomplish a particular purpose. Scripture gives examples of how the Spirit of God even came to unbelievers. In 1 Samuel 19, we have an account of how Saul was trying to kill David. He sent his messengers to bring David to him so he could kill him. Listen to what took place when these messengers found David:

18 Now David fled and escaped, and he came to Samuel at Ramah and told him all that Saul had done to him. And he and Samuel went and lived at Naioth. 19 And it was told Saul, "Behold, David is at Naioth in Ramah." 20 Then Saul sent messengers to take David, and when they saw the company of the prophets prophesying, and Samuel standing as head over them, the Spirit of God came upon the messengers of Saul, and they also prophesied. 21 When it was told Saul, he sent other messengers, and they also prophesied. And Saul sent messengers again the third time, and they also prophesied. 22 Then he himself went to Ramah and came to the great well that is in Secu. And he asked, "Where are Samuel and David?" And one said, "Behold, they are at Naioth in Ramah." 23 And he went there to Naioth in Ramah. And the Spirit of God came upon him also, and as he went he prophesied until he came to Naioth in Ramah. 24 And he too stripped off his clothes, and he too prophesied before Samuel and lay naked all that day and all that night. Thus it is said, "Is Saul also among the prophets?"

Every time Saul sent messengers to take David, the

Spirit of God would fall on them and they would prophesy. The Spirit of God even fell on King Saul when he went to get David personally so that he lay on the ground all night prophesying in the presence of Samuel. God's Spirit fell on these men of evil intent.

Some time ago I was involved in a Bible Correspondence ministry. People taking these lessons would send them in to me for correction. One of the questions asked in these lessons related to the assurance of salvation. The question was asked: How do you know you are saved? The individual responded by sharing how a few years prior to this she had been sick. She prayed that the Lord would heal her and He did. She assumed from this that she was saved. This was a big mistake. The Spirit of God may touch your life or even heal you from some sickness but this is not evidence that He set His seal on you to guarantee you a heavenly inheritance. When Jesus was on the earth, He healed many people. Many of those people still turned their back on Him. The Spirit of God may do something in you but this is different from the work Paul speaks about here in Ephesians 1:13-14.

Notice in Ephesians 1:13-14 that the Holy Spirit is given as a seal and a guarantee. In Bible times, a seal was used for two reasons. First, a seal was used to indicate ownership. A personal seal could be placed on an object to prove that it belonged to the person owning the seal. Secondly, a seal was used to make a legal document official. The seal confirmed the agreement and bound the individual to the terms of the agreement.

Paul is telling us here that when we came to faith in the

Lord Jesus and believed the word of truth, God entered into an agreement with us. Ephesians 1:14 tell us that this agreement relates to our inheritance and status as children of God.

Our heavenly Father seals this agreement with us by means of His Holy Spirit. In other words, He gives something of Himself as a sign of His commitment to us and to the inheritance He has promised those who believe in Him. In doing so, He legally binds Himself to us. Let's consider this thought briefly.

In Bible times, a document was usually sealed with wax and stamped with a special mark. That wax seal made a document official and bound the owner to keep his or her promises. God does not use a wax seal. Instead, His Holy Spirit literally comes to live in each believer. The presence of the Holy Spirit in our lives is the guarantee that God has bound Himself to us and will be true to His promises.

You, however, are not in the flesh but in the Spirit, if in fact the Spirit of God dwells in you. Anyone who does not have the Spirit of Christ does not belong to him. (Romans 8:9)

Notice that the Holy Spirit not only binds us to God legally but He is the guarantee of our inheritance. The word "guarantee" refers to an advance given as a security. When an agreement was made between two people; two things would happen. First, an agreement would be drawn up and signed (or sealed), making the deal official and binding. Second, a down payment was offered as a symbol of more to come. The Holy Spirit is the seal of God but He is also His down payment. God gives us something of heaven as a guarantee of what is to come.

As guarantor, the role of the Holy Spirit is to give us assurance that we are children of God.

16 The Spirit bears witness with our spirit that we are children of God, 17 and if children, then heirs— heirs of God and fellow heirs with Christ, provided we suffer with him in order that we may also be glorified with him. (Romans 8:16)

Notice how the Holy Spirit testifies or reassures us of our relationship with God and our inheritance as children of God. How easy it is to question our relationship with God. None of us are worthy of the inheritance He has promised. The Holy Spirit reassures us of our status as children of God and reminds us of the Father's commitment to us.

The apostle John taught this truth in 1 John 3:24 when he said:

Whoever keeps his commandments abides in God and God in him. And by this we know that he abides in us, by the Spirit whom he has given.

God's Spirit gives us the assurance that the presence of God is in us and that we belong to Him.

The seal and guarantee of the Holy Spirit are much more than the Spirit of God doing a work through us. It is nothing less than the presence of God in our hearts and lives. While we do not have the time in this chapter to consider all the benefits the Spirit of God brings to us, we understand from Scripture and hopefully from personal experience, that the Holy Spirit guarantees our inheritance in a number of ways. He reveals the Father to us and opens our minds to understand the things of God. He changes us from the inside and is shaping us into the image of the Lord Jesus. He protects us from the attacks of the enemy. He reassures us of our relationship with God and strengthens us to follow the path the Father has laid out for us.

Every believer has this seal of the Holy Spirit in their lives. This is what distinguishes us from the rest of the world. This is not to say that we always walk in tune with the leading of the Holy Spirit. We can certainly grieve Him at times. His presence will be evident to varying degrees depending on how willing we are to surrender to Him and His work. If you are a believer today, however, one thing is sure. The Lord God has sealed by putting His Holy Spirit in you. He does not leave you to fend for yourself. He gives Himself to you and promises to walk with you all the way.

The indwelling presence of the Holy Spirit is a guarantee of more to come. The presence of God's Spirit in us and the blessings He brings is a down payment on something even greater. Admittedly, our experience with the Holy Spirit has been limited. The fruit He produces in us is but a sample of what is to come. We experience joy as a fruit of the Spirit but as great as this joy might be, it is only a portion of what is to come. We experience a taste of fellowship with the Spirit and His leading in our lives but the day is coming when our earthly experiences will fade into deep and intimate communion that we have never dreamed possible.

The seal of God's Spirit in us is just a part of what God wants to do. It is a taste of something greater. It is a touch of heaven on this earth and a reminder that the fullness is yet to come. How much of God have we experienced? How much of His Spirit have we enjoyed? If we have not experienced even the fullness of our down payment, how much greater will be the richness of our inheritance?

If you belong to the Lord Jesus today, the evidence of this is the presence of God's Holy Spirit as a seal on your life. He comes as a rich blessing of heaven to our earthly lives. He comes as a taste of greater fullness to come. Open your lives to the work He wants to do in you. Open your heart to Him and let Him show you more of the richness you already have and the even greater richness of what is still to come.

For Consideration:

What is the difference between the Spirit of God using someone and the sealing of the Holy Spirit?

Can God use the unbeliever? Who is sealed by the Holy

Spirit?

What does the sealing of the Holy Spirit teach us about God's commitment to us and to giving us an inheritance in Christ?

In what way is the Holy Spirit a down payment on what is to come? What does your experience with the work of God's Spirit in your life teach you about what is to come?

Have you experienced the fullness of the down payment of God's Spirit? What keeps you from experiencing even more?

For Prayer:

Take a moment to thank the Lord for His radical commitment to us and to providing us an inheritance as His children.

Thank the Lord that He put His Holy Spirit in you as a guarantee of your inheritance and as an assurance that you belong to Him.

Thank the Lord for what the presence of His Spirit has been showing you about what is to come.

Ask the Lord to give you a greater understanding of your inheritance as you surrender more and more to the work of His Holy Spirit in you.

8 - MADE ALIVE IN HIM

4 But God, being rich in mercy, because of the great love with which he loved us, 5 even when we were dead in our trespasses, made us alive together with Christ—by grace you have been saved. (Ephesians 2)

As Paul begins Ephesians 2, he reminds the Ephesians of their condition before they came to know the Lord Jesus and the truth of the Gospel. He has five things to say to the Ephesians in this regard.

They Were Dead in Their Trespasses and Sin

Paul begins by reminding the Ephesians that before they came to know the Lord Jesus and the message of salvation, they were dead in their trespasses and sin (Ephesians 2:1). In other words, they had no spiritual life or power in them. We have seen that one of the blessings of being a believer is the seal of the Holy Spirit on our lives. The Holy Spirit comes to live in those who accept the work of the Lord Jesus on their behalf. What distinguishes the believer from the unbeliever is not so much what they believe or do but the presence of the Holy Spirit. The Spirit of God lives in the believer.

The unbeliever can do religious things but there are many religious people who know nothing about the presence of God in their lives. These people may have a deep concern for justice and integrity. They may be moral people and want to live a good life. They may have a love for the teaching of Scripture and seek to live according to its principles. To live a good life does not mean that we have experienced the salvation of God or know the reality of His presence in our hearts. To be religious does not mean that we are alive spiritually. Spiritual life is from God's Spirit who lives in the believer.

It is very easy to confuse religious belief and activity with spiritual life. We see someone who goes to church and assume that they are true believers. We hear someone who teaches the truth of God and assume that he knows the presence of God in his or her life. We are content with actions and beliefs when God wants to give us life.

Walked Following the Course of the World

Paul went on to say the before coming to know the Lord Jesus, the Ephesians walked according to the course of this world (Ephesians 2:2). They were unbelievers whose lifestyle was contrary to the teaching of the Word of God. They lived as they pleased with no concern for God or His ways.

Not all people who follow the course of the world do evil things, however. Some are very religious in nature and practice. We can do many things in the flesh. We can build large churches using proven business techniques. We can counsel our members to do what is moral and just. We can preach and draw large crowds. You don't have to be a believer to do these things. I am afraid that there are many people behind pulpits today who see great results in their ministry, are not alive spiritually. They are walking according to the principles of this life and not being led or empowered by the Spirit of God.

Followed the Prince of the Power of the Air

The third point Paul makes in Ephesians 2:2 is that the Ephesians, before coming to know the Lord Jesus, followed the Prince of the Power of the Air. The Prince of the Power of the Air is Satan. Paul is making a very bold statement here. He is telling the Ephesians that before coming to know Christ they were under the control and domination of Satan. This is the case for all who have never accepted the Lord Jesus. You may be a religious person but if you have never been rescued from the control of Satan you are still under his power. Jesus is the only way we can be released from the dominion of Satan. He alone was able to defeat his power and set us free.

Religion will not set us free from Satan or his power. In fact, the history of the church will prove that religious people are often Satan's most powerful weapon. Satan is not threatened by our religion or good works. He can use them to his end. He has often done great damage to the work of God by means of religious people who have never come to know Christ. The Ephesians were under the dominion of Satan. He controlled their destiny and held them in their sin.

Lived in the Passions of the Flesh

Fourth, Paul told the Ephesians that before they came to know the Lord Jesus they lived in the passions of their flesh. Paul was speaking particularly to the Ephesians here. It may have been that among them were men and women who had lived immoral and wild lives, satisfying the lusts of their flesh. There is plenty of evidence of people like this around us in our day as well. Before we dismiss this as not being applicable to our lives, we need to understand that the flesh is a powerful force. Who among us has not known fleshly temptation? This may come in the form of sexual temptation or immoral thoughts. It may also come in the form of ungodly attitudes. Admittedly, many people have been able to resist these temptations and maintain control of their actions but they are still very much aware of the power of the flesh and its passions.

Even as believers we are aware of the flesh and its temptations. There is an ongoing battle for our mind and body. With Satan's constant temptations and the sinful flesh crying out for satisfaction, the battle for purity is ongoing. Throughout the history of the world, people of many different religions have recognized this struggle. Men and women have disciplined themselves in an attempt to defeat these lusts and walk in a manner that is pure. Again, we need to be reminded that human efforts to discipline the flesh, though admirable does not guarantee that this individual has the life of Christ in them. We can be spiritually dead but tremendously disciplined and in control of our emotions and passions.

By Nature Children of Wrath

Finally, Paul reminded the Ephesians that before coming to know the Lord Jesus they were by nature, children of wrath (Ephesians 2:3). Sin separates us from God. All of us were born in sin. Without the forgiveness of Christ, every one of us was separated from God. This does not just apply to those who openly and willfully practiced sin in defiance of God's command, but also to those who tried their best to please Him. Our good deeds are not enough to save our souls. Our noble intentions are insufficient to give us a relationship with God. Satan had a legal hold on our lives because of sin. Only when the penalty for sin was paid and applied to my life would I be freed from the judgment of God.

Such is the life of all who have never known the salvation of Jesus Christ. They are spiritually dead, not knowing the life of God in them. They are caught up in the ways of the world because they do not know the leading and indwelling of the Spirit. They are under the dominion of Satan because they have never accepted the freedom offered them through Christ alone. They are entrapped by their passions. By nature, they are under the wrath of God and eternally separated from Him. While there is much more that could be said about this we must now turn to the focus of this study.

Paul told the Ephesians that one of the great spiritual blessings they had in Christ was that He gave them life. What is this life Paul speaks about? In the brief space that remains in this chapter, we can only touch on this important topic. The best way to understand this life is to contrast it with what Paul has been telling us in the context of this chapter about the condition of the Ephesians before coming to know Christ and His salvation.

What did the Lord do for the Ephesians when they came to know Him as their Lord and Saviour? The believers in Ephesus had been dead in their trespasses and sin. The presence of God or His Holy Spirit was not in their lives. They were under the condemnation of sin and would be separated for all time from God. They were unable to respond to God. They had no understanding of spiritual things or any real sense of their need.

The Lord Jesus changed the lives of the Ephesians. By paying the legal penalty for their sin Christ opened the door for the Spirit of God to work. The Holy Spirit drew them to Christ and sealed then by His presence in their lives. Something happened when the Spirit of God came to live in the Ephesians. Their minds were opened to spiritual things. The deadness of their heart was given life. In the place of emptiness and darkness, the life and light of God sprang up in them. They were aware of new power and desire in their life. With the forgiveness of sin came the sealing of God's Spirit. They became spiritually alive.

This new life of the Holy Spirit in them gave the Ephesians a completely new way of living. Once they were guided by human reason, now they were being led by the Spirit of God. His ways were very different from those of the world by which they had been previously guided. They found themselves walking in a whole new way. Once they depended on their own planning and experience. Now they found themselves trusting in a power that was bigger than them. In fact, they were put in situations that to all human appearances were impossible. In the strength of this new life, however, the impossible became possible.

The Ephesians, before coming to know the Lord Jesus, lived under the dominion of Satan. This was a dominion of darkness and death. Their only hope under his dominion was eternal death and separation from God. The work of Jesus Christ, however, rescued them from his grip. Jesus paid the legal debt and set them free from the dominion of death. Now in Him, they enjoyed the hope of eternal life in the presence of their heavenly Father.

As unbelievers, the Ephesians struggled with the passions of their flesh. They may have been able to control these sinful passions but the battle continually raged in them. Their city was filled with men and women who had been overcome by those sinful passions. Murder, immorality, dishonesty, and crimes of all sorts are the fruit of these passions.

When the Ephesians came to know the Lord Jesus and the presence of His Holy Spirit in their lives, something happened. They found that they were being changed from the inside. The Holy Spirit was changing their desires and passions. Something new and fresh was being produced in them. It is true that the old flesh was still present, but there was a life in them that was very different now. The life of the Spirit of Christ was overcoming the passions of the flesh. Desires were being changed as the Spirit of God shaped them into the image of Christ as they surrendered to Him. This was clearly a work of God's Spirit and not just an effort to control their passions. There was evidence of a life in them that was not natural. This life was changing them and giving them a whole new mind and heart.

No longer were the Ephesians children of wrath, heading for eternal separation from God. Now they were children of God, filled with His life and inheritors of His eternal kingdom.

The seventh great spiritual blessing we have in Christ is the blessing of being made alive. The Holy Spirit, by means of the work of Christ, gives us life. We are aware of the presence of God living in us. There is evidence of His presence in how we live and the way we think. His power is manifested in us and He guides us step by step into the purposes of the Father for our lives.

For Consideration:

How does Paul describe those who are without Christ?

What is the difference between being religious and being made alive in Christ?

What evidence is there of the presence of the Spirit of God in your life? What difference has God made in your life?

Is it possible for the believer to walk in the old ways of the flesh? What is the difference between walking in the flesh and being guided by the Holy Spirit?

For Prayer:

Take a moment to thank the Lord for the new life He has given you through the work of Christ and His Holy Spirit.

Thank the Spirit of God for the work He has been doing in your life.

Ask God to help you to surrender more and more to what He is doing in you through the ministry of the Holy Spirit.

9 - SEATED WITH CHRIST

4 But God, being rich in mercy, because of the great love with which he loved us, 5 even when we were dead in our trespasses, made us alive together with Christ—by grace you have been saved— 6 and raised us up with him and seated us with him in the heavenly places in Christ Jesus, 7 so that in the coming ages he might show the immeasurable riches of his grace in kindness toward us in Christ Jesus. (Ephesians 2)

As we continue our study of Paul's words to the Ephesians about their spiritual blessings in Christ we see from Ephesians 2:6 that we have been seated with Christ in heavenly places. There are several details we need to mention here.

Already Seated

Notice first from verse 6 that Paul speaks about being seated with Christ in the past tense. He "raised us up" and "seated us with Him." What Paul is saying is that, for the believer, this has already taken place. We are raised with Christ and seated with Him in heavenly places *now*. When did this take place? Paul told the Ephesians in verse 6 that they were raised with Christ. In other words, when Christ was raised, we were also well.

The resurrection and ascension of the Lord Jesus was not just a physical reality. It had tremendous spiritual implications. When Jesus died, He died for our sins. He died on our behalf so that the debt for sin could be forever paid. When He rose victorious over the grave, we rose with Him to eternal life. As Satan watched the resurrection and ascension of Christ, he was not only seeing the Lord Jesus rise to be with the Father, he was also seeing a whole host of believers, from every tribe and language rise with Him in victory over sin and the grave. The resurrection of Jesus gave us life as well. When He ascended to be with His father, we rose with Him spiritually and are seated with Him as victors and conquerors.

Admittedly, there will be a greater realization of this reality when we enter the presence of the Lord in heaven. Having said this, however, this should never keep us from the present experience of reigning with Christ on this earth. We are seated in a place of authority in Him. We are seated in a place of honour as children of God and inheritors of His kingdom.

Why we are Seated

Notice from Ephesians 2:4-7 the reason why we are raised with Christ and seated with Him in heavenly places. Paul tells us in verse 4 that because God was rich in mercy and loved us with great love, He raised us up and seated us with Christ. The Lord Jesus died, rose again, conquered sin and death and took us with Him into the presence of the Father out of pure love for us.

Notice also that we are seated in heavenly places "so that in the coming ages He might show the immeasurable riches of His grace in kindness toward us in Christ Jesus" (verse 7). Our Lord receives the glory for this wonderful kindness. He forgave our sin, raised us with Christ and seated us in heavenly places so that throughout all ages His kindness and mercy would be praised. We will have cause for all eternity to worship and honor Him for the "immeasurable riches" of His kindness in Christ Jesus.

What Does It Mean To Be Seated With Christ?

As we consider the question of what it means to be seated with Christ, the first thing we need to understand is that being seated with Christ has to do with our position or status as believers. We have been given a position of honor as children of God. This position brings with it certain privileges and obligations.

Security

Being seated with Christ places us in a position of great security. In Psalm 110:1, the Lord spoke to David and said: "Sit at my right hand until I make your enemies a footstool for your feet." Notice the invitation from the Lord here. He invites the king to come and sit with Him until He had conquered all his enemies. What a comfort that must have been for David in his time of need. There was no place as secure as the presence of God. What could harm him if he was seated with the Lord God? Who could touch him as long as he was seated in the presence of the Almighty?

Being seated with Christ we too can know this wonderful security. There in the presence of the Lord and under His watchful eye, we are secure. This is not to say we will not suffer or face difficulties on this earth. In fact, those who love the Lord often face persecution and trial. What we need to know, however, is that no matter what happens to us, because we are seated with Christ, the enemy does not have the final say. Our God is watching out for us. He has called us to His side to sit with Him until He has made every one of our enemies a footstool for our feet. To be seated with Christ is to be in a place of security.

Communion

Secondly, to be seated with Christ is to be in a position of communion and fellowship. Listen to what the Lord told His disciples in Luke 22:28-30:

28 *"You are those who have stayed with me in my*

trials, 29 and I assign to you, as my Father assigned
to me, a kingdom, 30 that you may eat and drink at
my table in my kingdom and sit on thrones judging
the twelve tribes of Israel. (Luke 22:28-30)

Notice that Jesus assigned the disciples a part in the kingdom so that they could eat and drink at His table. The eating and drinking that takes place here are not just to satisfy the needs of the body but also for the purpose of fellowship. We are invited to sit at the table of the kingdom of God in order to fellowship with our Lord. He delights to commune with us. To be seated with Christ is to be in a place where we can speak with Him and He with us.

God has given us life and opened the door for intimacy with Him. Who among us has not experienced this fellowship with Christ? As we are seated with Him, He shares His heart with us. We, in turn, share our burdens with Him. He listens to us and feels our struggle. We are blessed by His counsel. This is the privilege of all who are seated with Him.

Stewardship

Luke 22:28-30 speaks about the communion we experience seated with Christ. Being seated with Christ also places us in a position of responsibility. Let's look again at this passage:

27 For who is the greater, one who reclines at table or
one who serves? Is it not the one who reclines at table?

But I am among you as the one who serves. 28 "You are those who have stayed with me in my trials, 29 and I assign to you, as my Father assigned to me, a kingdom, 30 that you may eat and drink at my table in my kingdom and sit on thrones judging the twelve tribes of Israel. (Luke 22:27-30)

As Jesus sat with His disciples He did so as one who served (verse 27). He called those who sat with Him to act as judge (see Luke 22:30). Those who are seated with Christ have an obligation. With any position comes responsibility. God lifts us up and seats us with Christ so that we can be involved in the task of ministering and expanding His kingdom on this earth.

Every believer has been seated with Christ and as such has a God-given obligation. To be seated with Christ is not just for our own benefit but also for the benefit of others. God has called us to this place to use us for His glory. We are His ambassadors and servants. To be seated with Christ is to be called to a place of great honor but also to a place of great responsibility.

For each of us that responsibility is different. God has a role for all who are seated with Christ. He has called us each to a different task and has gifted us particularly for that task. We have an obligation to fulfill and we will be accountable to Him for the fulfillment of that obligation.

Authority

Those who are seated with Christ have been given His

authority. Paul reminded the Corinthians that they had been given authority in the Lord for the building up of the people of God.

> *8 For even if I boast a little too much of our authority, which the Lord gave for building you up and not for destroying you, I will not be ashamed. (2 Corinthians 10:8)*

To be seated with Christ implies carrying His authority. As ambassadors for Christ we speak in His name:

> *20 Therefore, we are ambassadors for Christ, God making his appeal through us. We implore you on behalf of Christ, be reconciled to God. (2 Corinthians 5:20)*

When we speak, we speak on His behalf. We minister in His name. He sends us and we carry His authority in our lives. Our association with Him and our calling give us this authority. We move in the power of His Holy Spirit to do what He has determined we should do. There is no greater authority. There is no greater responsibility.

We do not always understand this authority. We are often timid and fearful of what He has called us to do. Paul challenged Timothy in this regard when he wrote to him in 2 Timothy 1:6-9:

> *6 For this reason I remind you to fan into flame the gift of God, which is in you through the laying on of*

my hands, 7 for God gave us a spirit not of fear but of power and love and self-control. 8 Therefore do not be ashamed of the testimony about our Lord, nor of me his prisoner, but share in suffering for the gospel by the power of God, 9 who saved us and called us to a holy calling, not because of our works but because of his own purpose and grace, which he gave us in Christ Jesus before the ages began.

Paul reminded Timothy that he had been called and gifted by God for a purpose. He was not to be fearful or timid in his ministry but stand in the authority he had been given by God in his calling. To be seated with Christ is to represent Him and to carry with us the authority that comes with our calling as servants and ambassadors of His name.

Reward

Finally, to be seated with Christ is to be in a place of reward:

21 The one who conquers, I will grant him to sit with me on my throne, as I also conquered and sat down with my Father on his throne. (Revelation 3)

We are presently seated with Christ and given a place of security, communion, stewardship, and authority. The day will come, however, when our work on this earth is over and we will be rewarded with a place of honor at the Lord's side. There is a future aspect to being seated with Christ that we who remain on this earth have not yet known. As we overcome and walk in the authority He has given, there will be a reward for us. We will enter into a deeper and more intimate communion with Him. We will experience His presence as never before. The greatest reward for us as believers is to know Christ and to enter this deeper fellowship and intimacy with Him. This will be worth more than the mansions He has prepared or the golden streets on which we will walk. There in the presence of the Lord, we will know an even greater sense of what it means to be seated with Christ. Our experience on this earth is but a foretaste of something even greater to come.

Where are we Seated?

As we conclude this reflection, it is important to note that those who belong to Him are seated with Christ in *heavenly places*. This tells us something very important. In this world, the Lord Jesus was rejected and despised. He did not have a home or anything to call His own. To a worldly mindset, He died the death of a common criminal. He was a king but His kingdom was not in this world. He did not focus on obtaining this world's riches or treasures. These things did not interest Him. People did not understand Him or His ways.

In a similar way, we are seated with Christ in heavenly places. We may have nothing in this world to call our own. We may be rejected by those to whom we minister. Our authority is not from this world. Our methods are not of this world. Our rewards are not primarily here below. Our affections are in heaven. Our delight is in our Lord.

The Pharisees of the New Testament missed this point. They delighted in dressing in fine robes to be noticed by men and women of their day. They loved to be praised by human lips but did not concern themselves with the praises of God. As those who are seated with Christ in heavenly places, our focus is very different. We do not seek our reward on this earth. These earthly rewards mean little to us compared to knowing the smile of the Lord's approval. We persevere to please our heavenly Father and to receive His approval and delight. To do this, we willingly lay aside all we have in this life that we may obtain a greater heavenly reward.

To be seated with Christ is a concept that many people in this world will not understand. It is to be in a place of security, communion, stewardship, and authority. It is something we can experience on an ongoing basis in our lives on this earth. It is also something we look forward to experiencing in a deeper level when we enter the presence of our Lord in heaven to receive our reward. As those who are seated with Christ, we have the privilege of knowing Him and walking with Him in His power and authority on this earth. The question we need to ask ourselves is this: Have we entered fully into this privilege?

For Consideration:

What evidence is there in your life that you are currently seated with Christ in heavenly places?

What comfort have you received from being seated with Christ?

What obligations has being seated with Christ given you?

How does being seated with Christ give us a greater boldness in service?

What is the difference between being seated with Christ in heavenly places and having a place of honor in this world?

How does being seated in heavenly places change our perspective and focus?

For Prayer:

Take a moment to thank the Lord for the way He has been pleased to seat you in heavenly places in Christ.

Ask the Lord to help you to understand your privilege and obligation as one who is seated in heavenly places.

Ask the Lord to help you to have a focus on heavenly things and not on the things of this world.

Ask the Lord to help you to walk like a person who has been seated with Christ in heavenly places. Pray that this calling would be evident in your life to the glory of His name.

10 - CREATED FOR GOOD WORKS

For we are his workmanship, created in Christ Jesus for good works, which God prepared beforehand, that we should walk in them. (Ephesians 2:10)

God has a purpose in what He does. This is especially true when it comes to the matter of our salvation. We have been forgiven and seated with Christ for a special purpose. Paul told the Ephesians that they were the workmanship of God prepared for good works. There are some important truths we need to consider in this next great spiritual blessing we have in Christ.

His Workmanship

Notice that Paul told the Ephesians that they were God's workmanship. There is something very wonderful about this thought. I remember speaking to a doctor about the complexity of the human body. He told me how it was designed to work perfectly. Nothing was out of place. Every part of our body has a very specific purpose. Consider how the human eye is able to take in images that are relayed to the brain and interpreted in fractions of a second. This doctor told me that the material that makes up our body could be purchased very cheaply but the technology that makes these simple pieces work together is more than we could ever pay.

As I look around me on the island where I live, I see the beauty of God's creation. My eyes take in the images of the mountains and the ocean. My sense of smell takes in the aroma of the flowers. I feel the wind on my face. I feel the warmth of the sun. I can share these experiences with others as I speak to them. I could go on and on about this but suffice it to say that my body is a very complex organism. There has never been anything like it. It is the workmanship of an incredible God whose mind is beyond anything we could ever imagine.

The human body demonstrates the wonderful art and wisdom of God. We are designed by an infinitely wise God. Our bodies, in all their complexity, are marvels to behold and an amazing testimony to the skill and creativity of our Maker. This is not without purpose.

Created "In Christ Jesus"

It is important for us to understand that while the human body is a marvelous demonstration of God's workmanship, Paul's focus here is not on our physical body but on what we have become "in Christ." Notice that Paul tells the Ephesians that they were God's workmanship "created in Christ Jesus." It is true that the Lord Jesus was present and involved in the creation of the world (see John 1:1-2). We owe our existence to Him. The focus of the phrase "created in Christ Jesus" however, is more on the spiritual work of Christ in our lives. The phrase "created in Christ Jesus" is an important one. As marvelous as our physical life is, there is something even more wonderful about the spiritual life we have received in Christ.

This concept of being created in Christ Jesus is a difficult one for many people to understand. There are two reasons for this.

Many have never experienced this reality

All around us are men and women who have never experienced new life in Christ. Some of these men and women worship on Sunday morning. They enjoy reading the Bible and understanding the truth it contains. They discipline themselves to walk according to the truth of the Scriptures and do their best to serve the Lord. While all these things are admirable, they are being done in human effort. These men and women have never experienced the new life promised to all who come to Christ. Their religious life is a human effort to please God in the flesh. They do not know the power of God. They have never experienced the new birth.

Others have never experienced the fullness of this reality

The second reason why it is difficult for us to understand the phrase "created in Christ Jesus" is that many who have experienced new life in Christ have never experienced the fullness of this reality. For many years after coming to know the Lord Jesus as my Savior, I lived my Christian life in the flesh. I was not experiencing true intimacy with God nor was I experiencing His power in my ministry. I lived my life as if I had to do everything. I prayed but lived as if my organizing and planning were the real answer. I preached and felt that the power was in how I worded my sentences or in the way I presented myself. I hindered the leading and empowering of the Spirit of God because I trusted my own wisdom and gifting more than I trusted God and His Spirit in me.

How can we ever truly understand what it means to be "created in Christ Jesus" if we insist on doing things in our own strength and wisdom? Until we realize we cannot live the life God requires in the flesh, we will always fall short of God's purpose. Understanding the fullness of what it means to be "created in Christ Jesus" requires the surrendering of our lives to Christ and His work in us. We need to allow God to change us and shape us into the image of His Son. What Jesus did on the cross was only the beginning of the work God wanted to do in our lives.

17 Therefore, if anyone is in Christ, he is a new creation. The old has passed away; behold, the new has come. 18 All this is from God, who through Christ

*reconciled us to himself and gave us the ministry of
reconciliation. (2 Corinthians 5)*

From our salvation onward the Lord God begins to
form the character of Christ in us. His Holy Spirit
produces His fruit in our lives. We are being changed
from the inside. This is not a work of the flesh but
a powerful demonstration of the work of God's Spirit
as we surrender to Him. We know the leading and
guidance of God's Spirit in our lives. He empowers
us in ways we never knew before. We become new
people with a capacity to know God and enjoy His
presence and enabling in our lives. This reality is more
wonderful than anything we experience in the flesh.
We are brought into fellowship with God. We become
co-workers with God in the expansion of His kingdom.
The power and presence of God are transforming our
lives and enabling us to live a whole new way. There is
nothing in this world that could ever compare to this
new walk and relationship with God. Men and women
before us have willingly surrendered their bodies to the
flames to know this Christ. They have given up their
families and their most treasured possessions on this
earth to experience His smile of approval.

For Good Works

Notice that we have been "created in Christ Jesus" for
good works. It is important that we see what Paul is
telling the Ephesians here. Notice that they were first
created in Christ Jesus and then they did the good

works. Many people get this wrong. They believe that if they do the good works then they can become like Christ. This is not what Paul is saying here. He is telling us that if we want to do good works the first thing that needs to happen is that we need to become a new creation in Christ Jesus. Only those who have become a new creation can do the works God requires.

When the Lord Jesus saved us from the penalty of our sins, He did so for a reason. We were saved from sins so that we could enter a relationship with God but also so that because of that relationship, we could serve Him on this earth. Our salvation brings responsibility. We were created for good works. These works fall into two categories.

Holy Living

The first type of works God expects from us as a new creation in Christ relates to holy living. God expects that we live lives that reflect His character in this world. Those who are in Christ walk as Christ walked. It is their desire to live lives of integrity and holiness. We were created to reflect God in all that we do. We are His ambassadors in this world of darkness. We shine as lights in a world of sin. God created us "in Christ Jesus" so that we shine with the light of Christ in this world. When people see us they see the image of Christ in us. We are not like the world. We have been "created in Christ" and reveal His character to all we meet.

Kingdom Building

The second type of good works we are called to do relates to the expansion of the kingdom of God on this earth. Those who have been "created in Christ" or made new through His work have a responsibility to work with Him in the expansion of His kingdom. God has given us spiritual gifts and callings. He has shaped us through the things we have suffered. He has called us to a specific role in the kingdom of God. He has called some to minister as pastors, encouragers or teachers. Others He has called to confront the evils of this world as evangelists or prophets. He has called others to supportive roles through their finances or the use of their practical skills. Some He calls to remain in their own country, town, and family. Others He calls to move to far away countries. God has a purpose, however big or small that may appear to be, for each one He creates anew in His Son. Not one of us is without a purpose. You were created for good works. You were created to serve the Lord in a special way.

Prepared Beforehand

Notice something else about these good works. They were prepared beforehand for us. There is something quite incredible about this statement. God has prepared good works for us to do. From the beginning of time, God had a purpose for my life. He knew what He had called me to do. He prepared me through the circumstances of my life. He placed me as a child in the right family and orchestrated the circumstances of my life to train me for the precise tasks He had called me to do. However, big or small we may feel that role is, we are an important part of what God is doing on this earth.

Is there a more noble profession than this? You may be a powerful man or woman on this earth. You may have more wealth and riches than you could ever use. You may have servants and all your heart desires but what is this compared to knowing that you were created in or through the work of Christ Jesus for a particular role in the expansion of His kingdom on this earth? How could the riches of this world compare to knowing God and walking in that purpose? Men and women of this world have filled their lives with all the riches and pleasures this world offers and found only emptiness in the end. We have a clear example of this in the person of King Solomon in the Old Testament. On the other hand, we have all met men and women who have nothing in this life but whose hearts and lives were full. For these men and women, there is a purpose to life more glorious than anything this world could offer. They were created in Christ Jesus to demonstrate the character of their Lord and to serve Him by being His instruments of power and light.

What a joy it is to know that God has already prepared these works for us. As we take our stand and begin to walk the path He has for us, we will see these things unfold before us. He will make the path clear. He will provide all that is necessary. Everything has been prepared beforehand. All that is required is that we walk in obedience and experience the blessing of His purpose.

Do you know what it means to be created in Christ Jesus? Do you know what it means to have a purpose in life? Have you known the power of His presence in you? Are you walking in fellowship with Him? If so, then you are experiencing one of this life's most incredible spiritual blessings –a relationship with God and a very clear purpose in life. May God help us to understand this blessing and walk in the fullness of the works He has prepared for us.

For Consideration:

Take a moment to consider the "workmanship" of God in the creation. What does this tell us about the Creator?

What is the difference between being religious and being a new creation in Christ?

What does it mean to be created in Christ Jesus? Have we fully appreciated what this means in our spiritual lives?

Can we do the good works God requires before we are created in Christ Jesus? What difference does being created in Christ Jesus make in the works we do?

What are the good works God requires from all who have been created in the image of His Son? What are the works He has been preparing for you? Have you entered into those works?

How has God been preparing you for the work He has called you to do? What is God's calling for your life? Answer this in terms of His call to holiness and His call to service.

For Prayer:

Take a moment to thank the Lord for His workmanship in your life.

Ask the Lord to open your heart to what He has for you. Ask Him to show you the good works He has prepared for you. Ask Him to help you to walk faithfully in those good works.

Thank the Lord that He has a very clear purpose for your life. Thank Him for the privilege of being His servant.

Take a moment to pray for friends and relatives who do not know what it means to be created in Christ Jesus. Ask the Lord to bring them to Himself.

11 - BROUGHT NEAR

13 But now in Christ Jesus, you who once were far off have been brought near by the blood of Christ. 14 For he himself is our peace, who has made us both one and has broken down in his flesh the dividing wall of hostility ... 17 And he came and preached peace to you who were far off and peace to those who were near. 18 For through him we both have access in one Spirit to the Father. 19 So then you are no longer strangers and aliens, but you are fellow citizens with the saints and members of the household of God. (Ephesians 2:13-14; 17-19)

As we continue in Paul's teaching about our spiritual blessings we see from Ephesians 2:13 that the apostle told the Ephesians that they had been brought near in Christ. This merits some careful consideration. Let's take a moment to consider what Paul is saying here.

Far Off

The apostle begins by telling the Ephesians that they were once "far off." God is holy, righteous and good. We are unholy and sinners. There is a great distance between God and His creation. As sinners, we cannot approach a holy God. He hates sin and must punish it. Before coming to know the Lord Jesus, the Ephesians were separated from God by their sin. Notice from Ephesians 2:14 that the distance between us was so great it required a peacemaker. Speaking about the Lord Jesus the apostle says:

> *14 For he himself is our peace, who has made us both one and has broken down in his flesh the dividing wall of hostility (Ephesians 2)*

Verse 14 tells us that there was a "wall of hostility" between God and His creation. We were at war with God. He called for holiness and righteousness. We chose to sin and rebel. He demanded submission, we declared independence.

In the days of Moses, God determined that He would destroy His people because of their sin. Only when Moses pleaded for then did God relent (see Exodus 32:7-14). When Korah rebelled against Moses in Numbers 6:31-35, God opened the earth and swallowed not only Korah but his followers and family as well. In Genesis 6:5-8 God sent a great flood to destroy the earth and all its inhabitants because of their sin and rebellion. Only Noah and his family were saved. God takes sin and rebellion very seriously. The differences between us and our God are so great they require a peacemaker, one who can bridge the gap between us.

The Cost of Being Brought Near

This separation from God was a serious matter that required a drastic solution. Paul told the Ephesians that they were brought near "by the blood of Christ" (verse 13). While we were at war with God, He was willing to offer His only Son to pay the penalty for our sins and to bring us into fellowship. Jesus paid a very high price for our redemption. He took on the form of a man and suffered all that we suffer. He was mocked and ridiculed by His creation. He ultimately surrendered His life and hung on a cross for us so that we could be forgiven. Through His work as a peacemaker, we can now be at peace with God.

The Result Of Being Brought Near

Notice what Paul told the Ephesians about the work of Christ and its result in their lives.

He is our peace (Ephesians 2:14, 17)

In Ephesians 2:14 Paul told the Ephesian believers that the Lord Jesus was their peace. There can be no peace with God apart from the work of the Lord Jesus. In Him, the "wall of hostility" has been broken down. By

His death on the cross, He removed the obstacle of sin by paying its penalty so that all who accept His work could be forgiven and restored to a relationship with the Father. Paul told the Ephesians in Ephesians 2:17 that the Lord Jesus came to preach a message of peace with God.

What incredible news this is! Jesus comes to offer peace with God. The hostility between us does not have to continue. The wrath of God does not have to remain on us. We can be restored to a right relationship with the Father. What peace this brings to our hearts. Jesus has become the peacemaker, bridging the gap between God and humankind. He has turned the judgement of God from us and restored us to fellowship with our Creator.

Access to the Father (Ephesians 2:18)

Paul went on to tell the Ephesians that because of the blood of Christ, they now had access to the Father (see Ephesians 2:18). The God who was far off now becomes very near. When Jesus died on the cross, the curtain in the temple was ripped from the top to the bottom. This was a symbol of what the Lord Jesus had accomplished by His death. He removed the barrier between God and humankind.

What does it mean to have access to the Father? The use of the term "Father" is important. To have access to the Father is to have access to all that a father does. There are three things a father provides for His children.

First, a father provides security for his children. This means that we have a place to run to in times of trouble.

We have a heavenly Father who will care for us in the midst of the trials and storms of life. We have a Father who will stand between us and the enemy protecting us when we are in trouble.

Second, a father provides for the needs of his children. A father will care for his children's needs. He will provide them with food, shelter and the necessities of life. Our heavenly Father will do the same for us. Listen to what the Lord Jesus said in Matthew 6:25-33:

25 "Therefore I tell you, do not be anxious about your life, what you will eat or what you will drink, nor about your body, what you will put on. Is not life more than food, and the body more than clothing? 26 Look at the birds of the air: they neither sow nor reap nor gather into barns, and yet your heavenly Father feeds them. Are you not of more value than they? 27 And which of you by being anxious can add a single hour to his span of life? 28 And why are you anxious about clothing? Consider the lilies of the field, how they grow: they neither toil nor spin, 29 yet I tell you, even Solomon in all his glory was not arrayed like one of these. 30 But if God so clothes the grass of the field, which today is alive and tomorrow is thrown into the oven, will he not much more clothe you, O you of little faith? 31 Therefore do not be anxious, saying, 'What shall we eat?' or 'What shall we drink?' or 'What shall we wear?' 32 For the Gentiles seek after all these things, and your heavenly Father knows that you need them all. 33 But seek first the kingdom of

God and his righteousness, and all these things will be
added to you.

As a loving heavenly Father, the Lord God will care for
us and provide all we need. When we have a need, we
can come to Him and know He will care for us.

Third, the father loves his children. Sometimes this
world can be a cruel place. Especially as believers, we
will often face the opposition of those who do not know
our God. There will be times when we will need to
know the loving comfort and assurance of our heavenly
Father. There will be times when we will have to run
to Him and pour out our burdens. He will listen to us.
He will care for us. He will love us. When everyone else
turns from us we can be assured of His love. He will
always have time for us. He longs for us to come to Him.
His arms are always open to receive us.

What a privilege it is for us to have access to such
a father. Remember that there was a wall of hostility
between us but, because of the blood of Christ, that wall
has been broken down and now we can enter into the
presence of a loving Father.

No longer strangers but citizens and members of the household of God (Ephesians 2:19)

Notice finally that Paul told the Ephesians that because
of the blood of Christ they were no longer strangers
but citizens and members of the household of God

(Ephesians 2:19). The work of Christ did much more than forgive our sins and restore peace with God. It made us citizens of heaven and members of God's family.

As citizens of heaven, we have hope. The trials and pains of this earth will give way to a glorious future in the presence of God where there will be no more tears (see Revelation 21:4). We will live in the presence of God in a world freed from the impact of sin and evil. We shall know the joy of His presence for all eternity.

At one time we were enemies to God. Now through the blood of Christ, we have been brought near. This is not something we need to wait until we get to heaven to experience. We can experience elements of this wonderful nearness even now. We have moved from condemnation to fellowship and from hostility to delight in our heavenly Father's presence. We do not fully appreciate this in this life. It may not be until we enter His presence that we will fully understand that incredible blessing it is to be brought near to God in such a way. May God teach us, however, to delight in this nearness even now.

For Consideration:

What does it mean to be separated from God? How does Paul describe this separation in Ephesians 2:13-19?

What is the result of separation from God? What is the solution to this separation?

How does the blood of Christ bring us near to God?

What is the result of being brought near to God through the work of Christ?

Do we fully appreciate what Christ has done for us in bringing us near to the Father?

What does it mean to have access to the Father? Have you experienced this relationship with your heavenly Father? Give some examples.

For Prayer:

Take a moment to thank the Lord Jesus for His work which brought you near to the Father.

Thank the Father for the privilege of being His child. Take a moment to thank Him for some specific ways you have experienced His security, provision, and love.

Ask the Lord to help you to appreciate more fully what it means to be brought near to the Father. Ask Him to give you the grace to draw nearer still.

12 - A HOLY TEMPLE

20 built on the foundation of the apostles and prophets, Christ Jesus himself being the cornerstone, 21 in whom the whole structure, being joined together, grows into a holy temple in the Lord. 22 In him, you also are being built together into a dwelling place for God by the Spirit. (Ephesians 2)

In Ephesians 2:20-22 Paul compares the Ephesians to a great temple. He begins by speaking about the foundation on which they were built. In verse 20, Paul told them that they were built on the foundation of the apostles and prophets.

A foundation is very important for a building. It provides a solid base on which to build. With a solid foundation, the builders can build with confidence. Those who live in the house can be secure, knowing they are safe.

For our personal lives, a good foundation is also very important. The foundation we speak about here relates to our purpose and the criteria on which we base our decisions in life. People build their lives on many different foundations. We have met individuals whose foundation was materialism. These individuals build their lives on what will give them more money or make them more comfortable. This becomes the basis on which their decisions are made. I have met believers who have had this foundation in their lives. I remember speaking to a pastor whose decision about whether to go to a church was based on how much money they would give him.

We can build our lives on many different foundations. Some people base their lives on gaining acceptance and spend their energy in an effort to be approved by other people. This becomes the filter through which all decisions are made. I have also met individuals whose energy is focused on trying to prove to themselves that they are valuable. They push themselves to accomplish great goals in life to prove they are as good as someone else. Others have a foundation of pleasure. For them, life is about having a good time. The list can go on.

Not all foundations are equal. Some foundations will crumble and leave us in ruins. Many men and women before us have testified to this reality. We have all heard about men and women who have built their lives on seeking this world's goods and pleasures. We have also heard them testify to the emptiness this purpose brought to their lives.

Notice what Paul told the Ephesians in Ephesians 2:20. Their lives were built on the foundation of the apostles and prophets. These apostles and prophets spoke in God's name and communicated His will for their lives. The Ephesians lived according to what God spoke through these men of faith. The Scripture was the foundation on which the Ephesians based their lives. Every action was weighed in light of what God revealed in His Word through the apostles and prophets.

As we build our lives on the foundation of the prophets and apostles, we can be sure of God's blessing and presence. The storms of life will beat against us. There will be opposition and trouble, but our foundation will hold. We will stand before God one day, having built on this foundation and hear Him say "well done." What joy shall fill our hearts as we hear those words!

Christ the Cornerstone

Not only did the Ephesians have a good foundation upon which to base their lives, but notice also from verse 20 that the Lord Jesus was the cornerstone. The cornerstone was considered to be the most important part of the foundation. Some believe it was the first stone laid and the remainder of the foundation was built from it. As the foundation was laid, the builders would be sure that it was in line and level with the cornerstone. The builders needed that cornerstone in place if they were to build a good foundation. It was the starting place for the entire foundation and guaranteed that the remainder of the foundation was level and strong.

In a very similar way, Jesus is the starting point for us. He is the example we follow. He was the focus of the apostles and the prophets. Everything flows and is built from Him as the cornerstone. He has gone before us and set the example. We have seen His work. We have seen Him conquer sin and death. We have watched Him rise victorious over the grave into the presence of the Father. We have seen how He lived a perfect life, empowered by the Spirit. He is an example for us all. He is the stone from which our solid foundation is built. Because the foundation has a good cornerstone from which all measurements and decision are taken, we can be sure of its strength and reliability.

Joined together in Him

Paul continued in Ephesians 2:21 and explained to the Ephesians that not only were they built on the solid foundation of the apostles and prophets but also joined together in the Lord. Paul compares believers to a building in this illustration. Each believer is like a block in the great temple that is being built for the glory of God. There is something very wonderful about this.

We are not alone in this walk of faith. God has put together men and women of different backgrounds and cultures to form this temple. Each of us looks and thinks differently. We have different gifts and talents but we all have one common goal—to honor and serve the Lord God who saved us. We all have different roles to play but we all work toward a common end. The Lord God has joined us together through the work of the Lord Jesus. On this earth, we strive to serve Him and advance His kingdom. In the life to come, we will join hands in praise and thanksgiving forever in His presence.

The Lord has joined us together for a purpose. We are stronger together than apart. As we join hands, we encourage and strengthen each other. Admittedly, we do not always appreciate this fact. Sometimes our differences cause friction. That friction, however, is what grinds off the rough edges in our lives and makes us more like Christ.

Growing into a Holy Temple

Paul went on to tell the Ephesians that they were growing together into a holy temple in the Lord (Ephesians 2:21). Notice how Paul uses the word "growing." This word speaks of life. The temple which the Lord is building is alive. Not only is it alive but it is growing. It is growing in two ways.

First, the temple is growing in size. As the kingdom of God expands, more and more people are coming to know the Lord. They are becoming part of what God is doing all around the world. This kingdom of God is expanding despite the efforts of the enemy to destroy it. Each day, people around the world are coming to faith in the Lord Jesus and joining hands with us in this mighty effort.

Second, the temple is also growing in maturity in Christ. As each day passes, the Holy Spirit continues to shape each member of the temple more and more into the image of the Lord Jesus. We are being changed from the inside as the Holy Spirit works in us convicting us of sin and empowering us to be what God requires. He strengthens and matures us as He shapes us into this mighty temple.

There is something very fresh about the work of God. It is growing. It is alive. It is life changing. We are learning more about Him. We are experiencing more of His power and His person. We are growing in maturity and in closeness to our Lord.

Build Together into a Dwelling place for God by the Spirit

Notice how Paul concludes his thoughts in Ephesians 2:22. We are being built together into a dwelling place for God by the Spirit. Consider this for a moment. We are joining hands with men and women around the world for a purpose. Paul tells us that that purpose is to be a dwelling place for God. God is pleased to dwell among us. He is pleased to manifest His presence in our midst. He will reveal His glory through us. We are the temple where God will make His presence known.

This dwelling place is not in a physical building. The manifestation of God's presence on this earth is through His people. It is true that we do not always demonstrate the character and power of God who lives in us. We are growing in maturity, however. The Spirit of God continues to shape us and mould us into the image of the Son.

What is important for us to note from Paul's words here is that God is building a temple of human lives. Every day people are joining us in this wonderful work of God. He is building us on a solid and sure foundation. His desire is to build His people into a temple in which He is pleased to dwell and manifest His power, love, holiness, and glory. Could there be a greater goal in life? Could there be any greater reason to live?

For Consideration:
Paul told the Ephesians that they were built on the foundation of the prophets and apostles. What does this mean? How does this affect the way you live and the decisions you make in life?

What other foundations do people build their lives upon?
What is the cornerstone? How is Christ Jesus a cornerstone?

Paul tells us that we are joined together with other believers as members of the temple God is building. How have other believers been an encouragement to you?

How have you been able to work with others for the advancement of the Kingdom of God? Are there ways you can work better together?

How have you been growing in your walk with the Lord? What evidence do you see of God's presence in you?
Is the presence of God evident in the body of Christ in your society? Explain.

For Prayer:

Thank the Lord God for the sure foundation He has laid for us in His Word. Ask Him to help you to live your life on that foundation. Ask Him to keep you and your church from wandering from that Word.

Take a moment to pray for people you may know who do not have a sure foundation in their life. Ask God to reveal Himself to them.

Thank the Lord for brothers and sisters in the faith He has placed around you. Ask Him to help you to know them better. Ask Him to remove any hindrance to fellowship.

Thank the Lord that He is pleased to reveal Himself in you. Pray that His presence would be more evident in the body of Christ around the world.

13 - BOLDNESS AND ACCESS

11 This was according to the eternal purpose that he has realized in Christ Jesus our Lord, 12 in whom we have boldness and access with confidence through our faith in him. (Ephesians 3)

In Ephesians 3, Paul speaks to the Ephesians about his ministry as an apostle. He had been called by God to minister to the Gentiles showing them the way of salvation. These Gentiles were now equal partners with the Jews in the salvation that Christ offered by His death on the cross. They could come boldly into the presence of God through the work of the Lord Jesus Christ.

In Exodus 19:12-13, we read about how God called Moses up to the mountain where He would speak to him personally. While Moses was personally invited into the presence of the Lord God, the remainder of the people were to remain at the foot of the mountain. Notice God's warning to these people:

12 And you shall set limits for the people all around, saying, 'Take care not to go up into the mountain or touch the edge of it. Whoever touches the mountain shall be put to death. 13 No hand shall touch him, but he shall be stoned or shot; whether beast or man, he shall not live.' When the trumpet sounds a long blast, they shall come up to the mountain." (Exodus 19:12-13)

The presence of God was so awesome that no one was permitted to even touch the edge of the mountain. Anyone who did was to be stoned to death or shot to death with arrows. There was no way to get near to God. Only Moses had this privilege.

The people of God understood this greatness of God and His distance. The revelation of the glory of God was such that the people of God often feared for their lives.

And you said, 'Behold, the LORD our God has shown us his glory and greatness, and we have heard his voice out of the midst of the fire. This day we have seen God speak with man, and man still live. (Deuteronomy 5:25)

Even the priests, as God's representatives, were to be careful in their responsibilities lest they treat the presence of God lightly. There was a procedure and a time when God would allow them to draw near. If they disrespected this procedure they would be struck dead.

... and the LORD said to Moses, "Tell Aaron your brother not to come at any time into the Holy Place inside the veil, before the mercy seat that is on the ark, so that he may not die. For I will appear in the cloud over the mercy seat. (Leviticus 16:2)

A striking illustration of the danger of God's presence is seen in 1 Chronicles 13:9-10. Here we have the story of the Ark of the Covenant being transported on an ox cart. As the ox traveled it came to a certain place where it stumbled and the Ark of the Covenant risked falling off the cart onto the ground. A man by the name of Uzzah stretched out his hand to protect the Ark to keep it from falling. Listen to the result:

9 And when they came to the threshing floor of Chidon, Uzzah put out his hand to take hold of the ark, for the oxen stumbled. 10 And the anger of the Lord was kindled against Uzzah, and he struck him down because he put out his hand to the ark, and he died there before God. (1 Chronicles 13:9-10)

For daring to touch the Ark of the Covenant, Uzzah lost his life. There was a distance between a holy God and sinful man. To draw near to Him without invitation or in a way that dishonored Him was to perish.

When the Lord Jesus came to this earth, He came to deal with the problem of sin and how it separated us from God the Father. When He died for our sins and the penalty was paid, something very strange happened. Listen to Matthew's account of what happened when Jesus died to pay for our sins:

50 And Jesus cried out again with a loud voice and yielded up his spirit. 51 And behold, the curtain of the temple was torn in two, from top to bottom. And the earth shook, and the rocks were split. (Matthew 27:50-51)

Notice in particular that the curtain in the temple that separated the Holy of Holies from the rest of the temple was ripped from the top to the bottom. This was a direct result of the death of the Lord Jesus and the penalty for our sin being paid. God was showing His people that they now had access to Him because of what the Lord Jesus did on the cross. The barrier between God and humankind was removed and now, in Christ, we have full access to the Father.

Paul told the Ephesians that, because of Christ, they now had boldness and access to the Father. Let's consider what Paul is saying.

Boldness

Notice first that Paul told the Ephesians that they now had boldness before God. The word used here is the Greek word *"parresia"* which means, outspokenness, frankness or bluntness. It relates to freedom of speech where the person speaking communicates without reserve or fear. The idea is that we are able to approach

God and speak to Him honestly and without hesitation. The boldness Paul speaks about here is not just the ability to enter the presence of God, it is more than that. It is a boldness to communicate with God.

It is quite possible to be in someone's presence and not be in communion with them. An enemy may tolerate our presence but we have no relationship with him. This is not what Paul is referring to here. The boldness we now have in Christ is a boldness to communicate with God and enter a relationship with Him. We are now able to share our heart, our pains and our struggles with God. He invites us to such a relationship with Him.

Access

Paul also told the Ephesians that they now had access to the Father. The barrier of sin has been overcome. With the penalty for sin paid, we are free to enter the presence of God. Christ has made us acceptable to the Father. The Father opens His arms to receive us. He longs for us to come to Him. This is why He sent His Son to die. There in the presence of God is security, comfort, love and complete forgiveness. This is why we were created, to enjoy and honor our wonderful Creator.

Confidence

There are many people who feel that their sin is so great that they could never truly enjoy fellowship with God. Even believers hesitate to believe that they could truly experience the fullness of God's blessing and fellowship. Paul told the Ephesians that they could come to the

Father with boldness and confidence.

Those who hesitate to approach God and enter into deeper fellowship with Him have never truly grasped the deep desire of the Father for them nor have they fully understood the work of Christ on their behalf. God sent His Son out of love. He wants us to enter His presence. He has done everything to make this possible. Jesus has died so that every barrier between God and humankind would be removed. Nothing now hinders us from approaching God.

Paul tells us that we can approach God with confidence —confidence in what the work of Christ accomplished and confidence in the intense desire of God for us.

Through Faith in Him

Paul makes it clear that this wonderful privilege of approaching God is through faith in Christ (verse 12). This means that it is not about us deserving this privilege but about God's desire for us despite our unworthiness. We approach because of what Jesus has done for us. We approach because He has cleansed and forgiven us. We approach because God has opened His arms to receive us. We trust by faith in the work of Christ who made this relationship possible.

You may feel unworthy of this privilege but God calls you anyway. Will you hesitate to receive what Christ has for you? Will you be content with a God who is far away when He calls you to draw near? Will you be content with human wisdom and strength when the resources of an almighty God are at your disposal through Christ? There could be no greater privilege than that of drawing near to God, to enter a relationship with Him and to know the fullness of His fellowship. May this be our experience as we boldly and confidently draw near because of Christ.

For Consideration:

What is the barrier between God and His creation? How has this barrier been removed through the work of the Lord Jesus?

We spoke here of boldness as the ability to fellowship with God and speak openly with Him. Describe your relationship with God. What kind of fellowship do you have with God?

What is the basis for our confidence to enter the presence of God? Have you hesitated to draw nearer to God? What keeps you from deeper fellowship with God today? What is the invitation of God to you today?

For Prayer:

Take a moment to thank the Lord God that He sent His Son to die for the forgiveness of our sin.

Thank the Lord that He delights in our drawing near to Him. Thank Him that He listens to us as we share our hearts with Him.

Ask the Lord to give you greater boldness and confidence to draw closer to Him. Ask Him to forgive you for the times you have hesitated to draw near.

Ask the Lord to give you a deeper relationship with Him. Ask Him to draw nearer.

14 - PROVISION

20 Now to him who is able to do far more abundantly than all that we ask or think, according to the power at work within us, 21 to him be glory in the church and in Christ Jesus throughout all generations, forever and ever. Amen. (Ephesians 3)

I want to conclude this reflection of our spiritual blessings in Christ with Paul's benediction in Ephesians 3:20-21. There are several important details we need to consider in this benediction in the context of our blessings in Christ.

Paul draws our attention, in this benediction to what the Lord Jesus has done for us. Let's take a moment to break down what Paul is telling the Ephesians in verse 20.

Far More Abundantly

Paul begins in verse 20 with the statement: "Now to him who is able to do far more abundantly." The word translated "abundantly" is the Greek word "*hyperekperissou*" which in itself is a strong word. Notice the first part of the word "hyper" which is used in English to speak of something that is beyond the average or normal. The word "*hyperekperissou*" speaks of something that is beyond measure or exceeds all expectations.

Paul is not content to use this word "abundantly" by itself in verse 20. Notice how the word "more" comes before the word "abundantly". Paul is telling the Ephesians that the Lord Jesus is able to supply more than an abundance of all we need.

Notice again, however, how "more abundantly" is preceded once again by the word "far". The Lord Jesus is not only able to provide more than an abundance. He provides "far" more than an abundance.

We cannot miss what Paul is telling us here. What the Lord Jesus provides is beyond anything we could ever measure. His provision is way beyond our need. He has so much available for us that we could never measure it.

More Than What We Can Ask or Think

Paul went on to tell the Ephesians that the Lord Jesus was able to do far more abundantly beyond what they could possibly ask. The Greek word for "ask" is the word "*aiteo*" which means to ask, beg, crave, desire or require. Of course, this phrase needs to be kept in the context of the rest of Scripture. There are lots of things we crave or desire that are not good for us. This verse is not intended to be used in the context of satisfying our fleshly desires and lusts.

We need to see the feebleness of our prayers and human wisdom in what Paul is saying here. Paul told the Ephesians that the Lord Jesus was able to do far more than they could ever ask or think. Paul told the Ephesians that their greatest prayers were not equal to what God wanted to do. God would provide more than they could ever ask. He would do things through them they could never even think of doing.

The Power at Work Within

Notice, in verse 20 how Paul told the Ephesians that this power, that was able to do far more than what they could ask or think, was already in them. This power in them was not human strength and wisdom. Paul has made it clear that they could not even imagine what God could do. Their human wisdom was insufficient to comprehend the work and purpose of God. The power at work within them was from God. It was the power of the Spirit of God who came to dwell in the heart of the believer.

The question we need to ask ourselves is this. Am I in tune with the Spirit of God and what He wants to do through me? Am I experiencing something of what Paul speaks of here in Ephesians 3:20? Am I seeing God do things in my life that I could never have imagined? Am I seeing the victory of the Spirit over sin? Is my life bearing fruit for the cause of the Gospel that cannot be explained in human terms or by human programs and wisdom?

The truth of Ephesians 3:20 is very powerful. The power

of God is at work within us. He is able to do far more abundantly than we could ever ask or think. We stand back amazed at what God has done. Our hearts can only respond like Paul's by crying out:

To him be glory in the church and in Christ Jesus throughout all generations, forever and ever. Amen. (Ephesians 3:21)

What has happened though us is all of God. He deserves all the praise and glory. We cannot take any for ourselves.

What a privilege it is to be a child of God today. In the Lord Jesus, we have been abundantly blessed. The truths we have examined in this study are so basic that we can often overlook their richness and beauty. Each blessing we have examined deserves a book of its own. My purpose, however, is simply to highlight what Paul tells us about the blessings that are ours now because of Christ.

There is no excuse for weak Christianity. There is no excuse for timidity. In Christ, we have been abundantly blessed. We have all we need to be everything God has called us to be. Forgiveness, victory, and authority are ours if we belong to Christ. Provision, boldness, and leading are supplied in abundance. May God give us the grace to step out boldly in these blessings for the glory of His name.

For Consideration:

How does Paul's combination of the words, far, more and abundantly show us the measure of what God is able to do?

Are abundance and power seen only in big things? Can this power be seen in small and seemingly insignificant ministries as well? Give some examples.

Take a moment to consider how the Lord has blessed you. How has the Lord's leading and provision surprised you?

Where does all the power necessary for the work of the kingdom reside? Who is the source of this power? Are you experiencing evidence of this power in your life?

For Prayer:

Thank the Lord that He is able to do much more than you could ever ask or think. Thank Him for the times He has shown this to you personally.

Thank the Lord that He has put His Holy Spirit in our lives. Ask Him to help you to be more surrendered to the refining and empowering work of the Holy Spirit in your life.

Ask the Lord to demonstrate His power more fully in your life today. Ask Him to use you in an even greater way for the sake of His kingdom.

ABOUT THE AUTHOR

Light To My Path Book Distribution

Light To My Path (LTMP) is a book writing and distribution ministry reaching out to needy Christian workers in Asia, Latin America, and Africa. Many Christian workers in developing countries do not have the resources necessary to obtain Bible training or purchase Bible study materials for their ministries and personal encouragement.

F. Wayne Mac Leod is a member of Action International Ministries and has been writing these books with a goal to distribute them to needy pastors and Christian workers around the world. To date, tens of thousands of books are being used in preaching, teaching, evangelism, and encouragement of local believers in over sixty countries. Books have now been translated into a number of languages. The goal is to make them available to as many believers as possible.

The ministry of LTMP is a faith-based ministry and we trust the Lord for the resources necessary to distribute the books for the encouragement and strengthening of believers around the world. Would you pray that the Lord would open doors for the translation and further distribution of these books?

For more information about Light To My Path Book Distribution visit our website at www.lighttomypath.ca

Printed in Great Britain
by Amazon